TWO MEN
FROM EDEN

by
Morris Cerullo

Published By M.C.W.E., Inc.

First Edition April, 1977
Second Edition May, 1977
Third Edition June, 1977
Fourth Edition July, 1977
Fifth Edition August, 1977
Sixth Edition September, 1977

TABLE OF CONTENTS

Introduction

In the Beginning - And Before

Can two men walk together thousands of years apart?

Can two men have completely parallel lives though separated by 40 generations?

Can two have the same start with the same power and position and one utterly fail while the other is triumphant?

Can one man hold the keys to death while the other holds the key to eternal life?

Can we really know if there is life after death?

Can we really know what purpose there is to this life?

Can we really know if someone has established an unbreakable pattern for this world?

Can we really know if there is a personal God who concerns Himself with the day to day affairs of our lives?

Has something happened in your life recently that you are hard pressed to explain?

If so, perhaps it was a preparation for the experience you are about to have in reading this book.

Without presumption we believe that you are about to find the answers to some of the deepest, most probing, penetrating questions of your heart and mind.

The answers may not come from the source or in the form that you expected them, but *Two Men From Eden* may very well hold the answers you seek as we examine the devastating defeats of one. . .and the sweeping conquests of the other.

In some of the most majestic words of all time Moses declared simply: "In the beginning God created the heavens and the earth." (Genesis 1:1)

We take our cue from him:

Where better to begin. . .than in the beginning?

By His almighty power, God created the earth and brought all life into being.

The six days of creation are described beautifully in the opening books of Genesis. . .how God made light and separated it from the darkness and how He separated the heavens from the earth with the firmament. . .how He separated the waters to form the seas and the dry ground of earth.

Then came the creation of the vegetation and the luminaries, the sun to rule the day and the moon to rule the night. Next came the creatures of the sea and the fowl of the air.

Finally on the sixth day came the beasts of the earth and cattle.

After the first several days of creation, God began to assess His handiwork daily. At the end of each day's work, Moses related, ". . .and God saw that it was good." (Genesis 1:10)

That was the pronouncement upon the work of the third day, the fourth day, the fifth day.

The work of the sixth day was only *partially* completed when God ". . .saw that it was good." (Genesis 1:25). . . but creation was not yet complete. It was then that God revealed the staggering plan for His crowning creation:

> **Then God said, "Let Us make man in**
> **Our image, according to Our likeness;**
> **and let them rule over the fish of the**
> **sea and over the birds of the sky and**
> **over the cattle and over all the earth,**
> **and over every creeping thing that**
> **creeps on the earth."**

> **And God created man in His own
> image, in the image of God He created
> him; male and female He created them.**
> **(Genesis 1:26-27)**

In God's Image.

What a description of that creature. . .a description that certainly needs to be weighed.

If God made man in His image, does that mean that Adam's nose looked like God's nose? Does that mean that Morris Cerullo's eyes look like God's eyes or that your ears are like God's ears?

Of course not.

God is a Spirit.

He does not have hands like these hands of flesh, or feet like mine. He is a Spirit.

Therefore when man was made in God's image, he was made in the *spiritual* image of God.

Like God he has the ability to direct his own steps. He may choose his own paths. He can make his own choices.

God did not make man a puppet so that He could pull a string and man would lift his arm, or so that He could pull another string and man would shake his head. God did not make man so that by pushing a button He could make that man love Him, serve Him or obey Him.

What He did was to place within man God's own image which allowed man the privilege of choice. It gave him a free moral will power.

This freedom of choice is what makes it possible today for us to love God because we *want* to, not because He forces us to do so.

How would you like it if your son, daughter, wife or husband were a puppet and only loved you or responded to your love if you pulled the strings and forced a response?

The answer is obvious.

Neither did God want a forced response.

That is why He built into us a freedom of choice. He wanted our relationship to Him to be totally voluntary.

This freedom of choice, this moral will power, was God's image in Adam.

In man's spirit, God gave him divine authority and rulership over his own will. We often refer to this as man's free moral will.

It was a great gift from God. . .and yet that ability to choose is the very thing that the first Adam used *against* God. His capability to obey or disobey, bestowed as a blessing, actually became the instrument of destruction.

It opened the door on God's "good" creations and allowed "evil" in. It opened the door for sin, sickness and death to visit mankind.

It brought alienation between God and man, a wedge of division which was to be passed down from man to man through the ages.

We will see in these pages how no flesh escaped the devastation brought about through the first man's wrongful use of his right of choice, how no one has escaped the penalties of that first wrong choice.

BUT. . .

We will also see in these pages how even today God's will in us can work to the undoing of the very work which marred God's image in us.

Even today, thousands of years later, we still possess that God-image within us, that innate right of free will.

The same thing that caused Adam's downfall. . .is the very means which paves the way for our reconciliation to God.

The reconciliation is through a Second Adam!

It is the picture of these two men from Eden. . .the first Adam who brought us alienation from God. . .and the Second Adam through whom we have reconciliation to God. . .which we present to you in these pages.

Morris Cerullo

Morris Cerullo

Chapter 1

Who's Perfect?

God's crowning creation. . .

MAN!

Moses tells us that after God's creative work on the sixth day, after the creation of Adam, when God beheld the work of His hands:

> . . .God saw all that He had made,
> and behold, it was very good. . .
>
> (Genesis 1:31)

What was this "very good" creature like?

Perfect.

From every standpoint, he was perfect.

He was perfect in his creation, and perfect in the circumstances which surrounded him.

> **Then the LORD God formed man**
> **of dust from the ground, and breathed**
> **into his nostrils the breath of life; and**
> **man became a living being.**
> **And the LORD God planted a garden**
> **toward the east, in Eden; and there He**
> **placed the man whom He had formed.**
>
> **(Genesis 2:7-8)**

Perfection. . .innocence. . .beauty. . .health. . .dominion. . .luxurious setting. . .plenty. . .joy. . .communion . . .life. . .

. . . .and the amazing ability to reproduce life.

Take a look at man's first circumstances:

> **Then the LORD God took the
> man and put him into the gar-
> den of Eden to cultivate it and
> keep it.
> And the LORD God command-
> ed the man, saying, "From any
> tree of the garden you may eat
> freely;"**
>
> **(Genesis 2:15-16)**

> **And God blessed them; and God
> said to them, "Be fruitful and mul-
> tiply, and fill the earth, and subdue
> it; and rule over the fish of the sea
> and over the birds of the sky, and
> over every living thing that moves
> on the earth."**
>
> **(Genesis 1:28)**

> **Now the man had relations with his
> wife Eve, and she conceived and gave
> birth to Cain, and she said, "I have
> gotten a man child with the help of
> the LORD."**
>
> **(Genesis 4:1)**

The purpose of the creation of this marvelous creature
is pinpointed in Isaiah 43:7 KJV:

> **. . .for I have created him for my
> glory, I have formed him; yea, I
> have made him.**

God's great pleasure in His "very good" creature is ex-
plicit throughout the Scriptures. Prophet after prophet ex-
tols God's love for man not only in the beginning when
man was perfect but through the ages of imperfection and
failure which have followed.

Man was, and is, the apple of God's eye.

Moses spoke of this in Deuteronomy:

> . . .He encircled him, He cared for
> him, He guarded him as the pupil
> of His eye.
>
> (Deuteronomy 32:10)

David made it his prayer:

> Keep me as the apple of the eye;
> Hide me in the shadow of Thy
> wings,
>
> (Psalms 17:8)

This figure of speech encompasses not just one man, or even several. Just how encompassing is its scope is clearly illustrated in such portions as this one which refers to all of Zion:

> ". . .for he who touches you, touches
> the apple of His eye.
>
> (Zechariah 2:8)

A hint of the extent and the passion of God's love for mankind is held in the words of Isaiah 49:16:

> "Behold, I have inscribed you on the
> palms of My hands. . . ."

God's love for man expressed at this point and throughout the Tenach is all the more remarkable as it extends past Adam to a Chosen People and also to the whole human race because of what happened to Adam and. . . through him. . .to all mankind.

What makes it even more remarkable. . .to a degree that completely defies human definition and baffles the most learned mind. . .will be unfolded before us.

Here Adam stands then, made in God's image and pronounced "very good" in God's sight.

I believe that he stood straight and tall. His shoulders were not bowed with care. There were no cancers feeding upon his body. There was no emphysema choking his lungs. He had no allergies to prevent his utmost enjoyment of the vegetation which surrounded him.

Created perfect!

I have a saying I often use based on a truth I have learned. It is: "All truth is parallel."

For there to be light, and for there to be electricity, there must be a negative as well as a positive wire. One is not able to produce current without the other.

In order to bring us to that perfect understanding that we seek, to give us light, to restore us to *perfection*, we must deal with the *negative* that makes the *positive* necessary. . .the *imperfection* which demands the revelation of complete *perfection*.

Even with Adam's God-like qualities. . .with all of the advantages at his hands. . .all the pleasures at his disposal . . .with his privilege and right to walk upright in the very Presence of God and to hold perfect communion with God . . .Adam performed a negative deed which brought not only suffering upon his own life but disaster upon all mankind to follow.

This destruction came about through the very God-like characteristic he had: the right of choice.

With all the advantages, God gave man one single responsibility, one simple test of obedience, one unspoken appeal from God: "Obey Me because you love Me."

That simple test is outlined in Genesis 2:15-17:

> **Then the LORD God took the man
> and put him into the garden of Eden
> to cultivate it and keep it. And the
> LORD God commanded the man, say-
> ing, "From any tree of the garden you**

> may eat freely; but from the tree of the
> knowledge of good and evil you shall
> not eat, for in the day that you eat
> from it you shall surely die."

How Adam met this test, or rather how he failed it, is
the dismal negativism of Genesis 3:6:

> When the woman saw that the tree
> was good for food, and that it was
> a delight to the eyes, and that the
> tree was desirable to make one wise,
> she took from its fruit and ate; and
> she gave also to her husband with
> her, and he ate.

The effects of Adam's failure were both immediate and
far-reaching. They have touched every life which has ever
existed on this earth and. . .they are still reaching. His act
thousands of years ago has had a tremendous impact upon
you which you are still experiencing to this day. It will
continue to affect every person born in the future.

God had promised Adam that his disobedience would
bring death.

That is exactly what happened.

Adam suffered immediate spiritual death. He put to the
knife his initial innocence. He sacrificed for one morsel of
forbidden fruit the beautiful, open communion he had en-
joyed with God.

Another simple but awful reality is that physical death
also resulted from that first sin.

There is absolutely no way in the world to explain the
existence of death apart from the existence of evil. The
fact of death is otherwise totally unreasonable and completely defies any other explanation.

There is not a single scientific or medical reason why
man should die. Man was created to live. He was intended

to be a deathless being, living in fellowship with the living God forever.

Conceivably, the life-building processes could have gone on forever.

Why should man reach a certain point of physical development and then begin to deteriorate?

Why do the life-building forces begin to wane and fall short of their full goal?

There is only one explanation and that is the Bible explanation: Death is a consequence of sin.

Without sin, there would have been *change* but not *death*.

The construction of the universe is based upon the principle of the "Law of Kind."

Everything in God's creation reproduced itself "after its kind." Plant life produced plant life; animal life produced animal life; human life produced human life.

Adam was created in the image and likeness of God. Had he continued to be that "kind," he would have brought forth after that "kind."

However, sin defaced the image of God and destroyed His likeness in Adam.

Adam became another "kind." He was no longer in God's image and God's likeness. He had within him the image and likeness fashioned by his sin.

Moses is careful to point out that after the catastrophe of sin Adam "became the father of a son in *his* own likeness, according to *his* image." (Genesis 5:3)

This *Adam's* sin became *our* sinfulness.

Theologians and philosophers may argue about the exact meaning of the words "in the day that you eat from it you shall surely die," but the stubborn fact remains, ". . .it is appointed for men to die once, and after this comes judgment. . . ." (Hebrews 9:27)

In the eloquent words of Solomon, "It is the same for all." (Ecclesiastes 9:2)

To put it in modern statistics: "The death rate is every one out of one."

A SURE RENDEZVOUS

All of mankind must echo the poetic words of Alan Seeger, words written just before Seeger's tragic death in World War I: "I have a rendezvous with death/At some disputed barricade/. . .And I to my pledged word am true/I shall not fail that rendezvous."

As the story of man unfolds in the Book of Genesis, one phrase is repeated with the solemnity of the tolling of bells . . ."and he died." Over and over we read the record of a man's progeny, followed by the awesome words "and he died."

No matter how assured of life a man might seem to be, there comes to every person sooner or later a moment when the death bell tolls the message. . ."and he died."

Sin, broken communion with God, and finally, death became the penalty upon all flesh through Adam's disobedience.

Adam, having passed on, left us his earthly heritage.

One writer has described this heritage in this graphic manner:

> . . .by one man sin entered into
> the world, and death by sin; and
> so death passed upon all men,
> for that all have sinned:
>
> **(Romans 5:12 KJV)**

> . . .by one man's disobedience
> many were made sinners. . .

> **(Romans 5:19 KJV)**

> . . .in Adam all die. . .

> **(I Corinthians 15:22 KJV)**

At this point in time, God's great love for man and the absolute righteousness of His character seemingly placed God in an insoluble dilemma:

His righteous judgment demanded death and banishment for the sinner. God cannot look upon sin.

At the same time His love cried out to confer compassion and forgiveness and restoration.

How could He possibly satisfy one demand of His character without violating the other?

Was there. . .*is* there. . .an answer?

Perhaps a Second Adam's obedience may hold the key?

Chapter 2

The Search for Answers

Adam sinned.

The question now is this:

If God loves man as has been indicated to us, how can He possibly condemn man?

And if God is true and not a liar, how can He possibly not pronounce judgment?

The dilemma is clear: God's *love* must be satisfied, and God's *judgment* must be satisfied.

Is there a way to accomplish this?

God's answer is at once both simple and profound:

God Himself would supply a substitute so that His judgment might be satisfied, and yet His love might continue to be visited upon His crowning creation.

He at once puts into motion His great plan of redemption.

Even before Adam and Eve were expelled from the Garden of Eden because of their sin, a loving and merciful God had already made provision for their return to fellowship with Him on the grounds of atonement through the sacrificial blood of a lamb.

When God came down to commune with Adam in the cool of the evening as had been His custom, He found Adam hiding among the trees with the feeble excuse that he had realized he was naked and had hid himself.

Adam and Eve's effort to cover their nakedness with fig leaves was not sufficient. God Himself slew an animal and clothed them with the skins.

> **And the LORD God made gar-**
> **ments of skin for Adam and**
> **his wife, and clothed them.**

(Genesis 3:21)

This was to become the first blood sacrifice to atone for man's sin. Many more such sacrifices were to follow after Adam left the Garden and through the generations to follow. . .but even this was not the ultimate answer.

In His great mercy and concern, God voiced that ultimate answer even before banishing Adam and Eve from the Garden.

Oh, it is true that they were punished for their sin.

Hereafter Adam would have to earn his living by the sweat of his brow. Hereafter, woman would know the pangs of childbirth. Hereafter the earth would be cursed with briers and thorns. Hereafter the serpent must crawl on his belly in the dust. Hereafter they would be banished from Eden and the way barred so that they could not eat of the Tree of Life and live forever in their sinful condition. . . .

But even while these judgments were still fresh from the lips of God, He uttered one of the most significant statements He ever made.

It is found in these tremendous words spoken to the serpent (Satan).

> **And I will put enmity Between**
> **you and the woman, And be-**
> **tween your seed and her seed;**
> **He shall bruise you on the**
> **head, And you shall bruise**
> **him on the heel."**

(Genesis 3:15)

Here the way back to God is revealed. The Seed of the woman, One born of the woman, would appear on the human scene and destroy the works of the devil who had snared our first parents into sin.

From the third chapter of Genesis, the Bible becomes a book recording a two-fold story of man:

It is the history of evil which resulted from man's disobedience.

And it is the history of redemption as the way is opened for sinful man to return to his God.

In order for Adam and Eve to appear again in the presence of God, it was necessary that their nakedness be covered. It was for this reason that God made for them coats of skins; the fig-leaf covering they had contrived for themselves was not acceptable. *Acceptable* clothing cost the life of an innocent lamb.

Two great facts about redemption emerge in this third chapter of Genesis.

One: Redemption is costly. Atonement is made by the shedding of the blood of the lamb. The innocent lamb died in the stead of and for the sake of the guilty. Because of the shed blood, a coat of skins provided clothing for the guilty so that they might stand before God, covered!

Two: Redemption is to be accomplished through the work of One born of the woman - the Seed of the woman.

Let me reiterate these two great facts of redemption. Redemption's cost is paid for in the blood of the innocent lamb. . . .Redemption is accomplished through a Person.

EVE'S MISTAKE

Now the man had relations with his wife Eve, and she conceived and gave birth to Cain, and she said, "I have gotten a manchild with the help of the LORD."

(Genesis 4:1)

Eve gave birth to her first son and her words after his birth are worthy of special attention. Her ecstatic utterance reveals how clearly she grasped the meaning of the original promise in Genesis 3:15.

Literally rendered, she exclaimed, "I have gotten a man, even the Lord."

The Jerusalem Targum renders it even more forcefully, "I have gotten a man, the Angel of the Lord."

Though it may be argued that the expression "Angel of the Lord" is not introduced until the patriarchal history, the strength of what Eve meant is reinforced.

The critical importance of Eve's words indicate that she understood that "the Seed" promised in the third chapter referred to a supernatural entrance of the Lord into the human sphere.

Eve believed that Cain was the promised Seed, but she was mistaken. Cain was not that Seed.

However, Eve was not mistaken in her *concept* that this was how the Messiah, the Seed of woman would appear on the human scene.

CAIN'S MISTAKE

And again, she gave birth to his
brother Abel. And Abel was a
keeper of flocks, but Cain was a
tiller of the ground. So it came
about in the course of time that
Cain brought an offering to the
LORD of the fruit of the ground.
And Abel, on his part also brought
of the firstlings of his flock and of
their fat portions. And the LORD
had regard for Abel and for his
offering;

(Genesis 4:2-4)

Have you ever wondered why Cain's offering was not accepted? It was, after all, a beautiful offering. It was the fruit of the earth, and it represented the fruit of his toil.

But in making this kind of an offering:

1. Cain denied that sin had separated him from God.

2. Cain denied the need of reconciliation to God.

3. Cain denied that he needed the death of a substitute.

4. Cain denied the idea that the ground was cursed.

5. Cain insisted that the fruit of the ground, and the fruit of his labor should be acceptable to God.

6. Cain denied that death as a judgment from God was upon him.

The meaning of Cain's offering has a familiar ring in our times for there are those who teach that:

1. Man is not separated from God by sin.

2. Death is not an evidence of God's judgment against sin.

3. Blood sacrifice by death of a substitute is not necessary.

4. Human nature is not under the curse.

5. Human nature is inherently good, and that by culture man can bring out of it fruit acceptable to God and society.

6. This fruit can be offered to God in the form of good works and good character.

Cain's offering was rejected because:

1. The ground out of which Cain took his offering had been judged and cursed by God.

2. In offering the fruit of the ground, Cain offered that which God had judged and condemned. Cain in effect denied God's Word.

Do these facts have meaning for us?

Human nature, like the ground under Cain's feet, has been judged and condemned of God.

In offering God our own righteousness, our own good deeds, we deny God's judgment, trample it under foot, and insult Him because we offer Him that which He Himself has condemned and refused. This means that every self-righteous man is walking in the way of Cain!

BRIDGING THE GAP

Abel's offering stands in sharp contrast to that of his brother, Cain.

Abel offered a lamb, and in offering a lamb in sacrifice, Abel confessed:

1. That he believed that sin had separated him from God.

2. That as a consequence of sin, death was a certain judgment of God.

3. That God's judgment against sin was a just judgment.

4. That God had provided a way of redemption through the blood of a lamb - a doctrine of atonement which had been taught to his parents, Adam and Eve, and which they in turn had passed on to him.

5. In offering the lamb, Abel proclaimed the righteousness of God's judgments and he also confessed his trust in the grace of God which provided atonement through the blood of the lamb.

GOD'S RESPONSE

> . . .Abel, on his part also brought of
> the firstlings of his flock and of their
> fat portions. And the LORD had re-
> gard for Abel and for his offering;
> but for Cain and for his offering He
> had no regard. So Cain became very
> angry and his countenance fell.
>
> (Genesis 4:4-5)

How did God respond to these two offerings?

He accepted Abel's offering and rejected Cain's.

Was it because Cain was a bad man and Abel was a good man? No!

The true answer is given in the words:

> By faith Abel offered to God a better
> sacrifice than Cain. . .
>
> (Hebrews 11:4)

The real difference was not in the men. Both were sons of Adam and Eve. Both were outside of Eden. Both lived under the curse and under the sentence of death.

The real difference was not in the men, but in what they offered. The blood of the lamb was the vital difference. Cain was rejected because he sought to come to God *without* the blood of the lamb. Abel was accepted because he approached God *with* the blood of the lamb.

Acceptance or rejection before God rested on the one great primary truth of redemption: a substitutionary sacrifice, the blood of the Lamb.

This was the difference between Cain and Abel.

This was the difference between the Egyptians and the Children of Israel on the night of the Passover.

This is the difference between those who are saved or lost now. It is the difference in redemption for all of Adam's sons and daughters.

OPPORTUNITY

In His grace, God spoke directly to Cain and offered him the opportunity to receive forgiveness. As He had manifested respect and acceptance to Abel for his offering, God offered the same to Cain.

God said, "If you do well, will not your countenance be lifted up?" (Genesis 4:7)

In other words, "Offer the right offering and you shall be accepted."

Abel's flocks of sheep were there right outside his tent door. . . .Had he brought a firstling of the flock as Abel did, it would have been accepted.

This was Cain's opportunity. If he had acted on it, how different his story would have been!

Here is where we can draw a big difference between these two men.

They came from the same parents, the same environment, the same background and training. . .but one found the way of truth. . .and the other did not.

In the search for answers, one must *desire* truth if one is to *find* truth, for many are the by-ways and dead-ends.

Solomon warned:

> **There is a way which seems right to a man,**
> **But its end is the way of death.**
>
> **(Proverbs 14:12)**

Both Cain and Abel had been instructed by Adam in the ways of acceptable sacrifice. Cain even received further instruction from God and was given another opportunity to walk in the way of true redemption. . .but he shunned the truth even when it was clearly shown.

I cannot stress enough how crucial it is that we maintain an honest, open heart in our search for answers. We must not try to make our own facts, or supply our own answers. God alone has the facts and knows the answers.

If we are to seek true answers and find them, our attitude must be that of the Psalmist David:

> **When Thou didst say, "Seek My face,"**
> **my heart said to Thee, "Thy face, O**
> **LORD, I shall seek."**

> **(Psalm 27:8)**

An honest, open, searching heart is the first step on the pathway that leads to all truth.

Chapter 3

The Road Begins

When Cain closed his eyes to the truth that God required of him the sacrifice of an innocent lamb, he also closed his eyes to the other truth of redemption. . .that it would be accomplished through a Person as spelled out specifically in Genesis 3:15.

I want to repeat that Scripture in its entirety because of its profound significance in God's overall plan of redemption. . .and especially as we begin to examine the Scriptures that would pinpoint Who that Person is.

> **And I will put enmity Between you and
> the woman, And between your seed and
> her seed; He shall bruise you on the head,
> And you shall bruise him on the heel."**

> **(Genesis 3:15)**

These words were God's pronouncement upon the serpent who was the instrument of man's disobedience. They immediately pinpoint both the story of sin and failure on man's part, and the story of redeeming love on God's part.

Here is the first promise ever given of a Redeemer. It came immediately upon the heels of the *need* for a Redeemer. At once God set in motion a plan whereby Adam and all the sons of Adam might be redeemed and restored to Himself.

What an amazing plan it is!

One born of the woman would appear on the human scene who would accomplish deliverance.

We have noticed that the Seed of the woman is, in the first place, referred to as "he," and the verse speaks of bruising "him" on the heel. . .making the Seed of the woman ultimately a single Person.

Genesis 3:15 thus becomes the first marker on the most famous highway known to man, the Highway of the Seed.

Each time God reiterated His promise concerning the coming Seed, another name was posted on that highway. Abel, Seth and Noah are to be found in Genesis 6:8-10; Shem in Genesis 9:26 and 27; Abraham in Genesis 12:1-4; Isaac in Genesis 17:19-21; Jacob in Genesis 28:10-14; Judah in Genesis 49:10; and David in 2 Samuel 7:15-17.

All of these progenitors are as markers pointing down the road which leads to the Messiah, the Anointed One, the Promised Seed. All the hopes of mankind rest on the fulfillment of God's gracious promise concerning the coming Deliverer.

As Adam was created in the image of God, an image he marred, these markers point to One who is the *express* image of God, One who will be obedient, One who will not fail, One who will effect the complete reconciliation of God and man. The One promised in fact was to *be* the image of God.

How is that possible?

It is possible because of the very nature of God.

God's instruction when He first announced His intention of creating man was "Let us make man in our image . . ."

We know that there is only one God.

Hear, O Israel: The LORD our God is one LORD:(Deuteronomy 6:4 KJV)

Who is the "us" included in God's work of creation? God is the only Creator. . . .How could there be an "us" without there being a co-creator?

To the finite mind there is no answer, but in God's mystical, heavenly arithmetic, the answer is quite simple:

God was speaking of Himself.

For the first time He is unveiling the triune character of His Being. . .One God, but three manifestations.

There is no dispute with the fact that God is a Spirit . . .and yet the Scriptures are full of His manifestation in visible form in a series of appearances known as "theophanies." These divine appearances were witnessed by such creditable witnesses as Moses, Abraham, Isaac, Jacob and Gideon.

The Jewish Star of David speaks to us of the triune nature of God as well as of the triune nature of man. The upper triangle, representing God, is illustrative of the Father, Messiah and Holy Spirit, while the lower triangle, pointing downward, speaks of man's trinity. . .body, soul and spirit.

That the Promised One or Messiah would be of divine origin is borne out throughout the Scriptures.

From earliest time, man sought to bring about reconciliation with God through sacrifices of the blood of sheep and goats. . .but this was just an imperfect foreshadow to be repeated year after year until the Perfect One, the true Redeemer, would come whose sinlessness would suffice for all time. . . .One who would be the express image of God in a unique way.

While this Second Adam is a mystical Person, yet we have many clues and we know much about Him. The road signs, though often blurred by obscure language, nevertheless become amazingly clear in the light of a searching heart.

God spoke clearly of the miraculous Person to come from the very first. Genesis 3:15 is but the forerunner of many another such treasure sign placed with frequency throughout the Tenach.

Micah told exactly *where* this Person would be manifested:

> "But as for you, Bethlehem Ephrathah,
> Too little to be among the clans of
> Judah, From you One will go forth
> for Me to be ruler in Israel. His goings
> forth are from long ago, From the days
> of eternity."
>
> (Micah 5:2)

Genesis 49:10 tells us the very *tribe* from which He would come:

> "The scepter shall not depart from
> Judah, Nor the ruler's staff from be-
> tween his feet, Until Shiloh comes,
> And to him shall be the obedience of
> the peoples.
>
> (Genesis 49:10)

Daniel gives us the *time* of His coming:

> "So you are to know and discern that
> from the issuing of a decree to restore
> and rebuild Jerusalem until Messiah
> the Prince there will be seven weeks
> and sixty-two weeks;. . ."
>
> (Daniel 9:25)

The total of 69 weeks is interpreted by the leading scholars almost without exception as a total of 483 years.

Though there were many decrees concerning the walls and the temple, only one specifically designated the city. That came from Artaxerxes to Nehemiah on the first day of Nisan in the year 445 B.C.

> And I said to the king, "If it please
> the king, and if your servant has found
> favor before you, send me to Judah,
> to the city of my fathers' tombs,
> that I may rebuild it."
>
> (Nehemiah 2:5)

Converting the lunarsolar year into days (360) times 483 years mentioned as the span of the time until the appearance of Messiah, the seeker will arrive at the 10th day of Nisan in the 18th year of Tiberias Caesar.

By these calculations, that should have been a most important day in the history of mankind!

Indeed, the whole story of the Bible leads inexorably to the Anointed One.

Each great crisis in the story of man called for a human channel God could use. God always raised up a man through whom He re-confirmed His promise of the coming Seed of the woman. The chain of promises and prophecies forms a clear path which leads from the third chapter of Genesis directly to the One Who will stand in relation to man as did Adam. . .a Second Adam. . .but with an important difference:

Whereas the first Adam failed, the Promised One, the Second Adam triumphed!

Whereas the first Adam failed through disobedience to the divine will of God, the Second Adam triumphed through His perfect obedience.

Prophets through the ages developed the image of the Deliverer-from-sin Who was to come and be revealed clearly as the Son of God, called the Messiah.

The One Who could claim the position of the Messiah would have to have many of the same characteristics that the first Adam had. This is because the Second Adam, or the Messiah, would have to overcome in the same specific points where the first Adam failed if He is to reconcile the alienated creature to the Creator.

Moreover, He would have to have the exact lineage and genealogy spelled out in the Scriptures. Even one variation would void the claim completely.

Scholars tell us that there are 333 definite prophecies

in the Old Testament which keenly pinpoint the qualifications of the Messiah. A person could not meet 332 of the conditions and still qualify. Only perfection, absolute compliance with all 333 prophecies, would prevail.

Down through the ages, there have been many who have claimed to be the Messiah.

There have been some in every age. We can call the names of some in the recent past. There are some walking the earth even today who claim to be the Messiah.

Has a single one of these claims ever proved valid?

Has there been One who has met every prophecy, fulfilled every lineage requirement, coincided with every guidepost, triumphed in every area in which the first Adam failed?

If so, if there has been One like that, He would not only be a Person, the Seed of a woman, but He also would be that perfect Sacrifice which is the only ultimate atonement from sin: The two aspects of redemption united in one Being. . .an innocent sacrificial Lamb. . .and a Person, born of a woman.

Such a One is described in these stirring words from the prophet Isaiah:

> **Who has believed our message? And
> to whom has the arm of the LORD
> been revealed? For He grew up be-
> fore Him like a tender shoot, And
> like a root out of parched ground;
> He has no stately form or majesty
> That we should look upon Him.
> Nor appearance that we should be
> attracted to Him. He was despised
> and forsaken of men, A man
> of sorrows, and acquainted with
> grief; And like one from whom**

men hide their face, He was des-
pised, and we did not esteem
Him. Surely our griefs He Himself bore, And our sorrows He
carried; Yet we ourselves esteem-
ed Him stricken, Smitten of God,
and afflicted. But He was pierced
through for our transgressions,
He was crushed for our iniquities;
The chastening for our well-being
fell upon Him, And by His scourging we are healed All of us like
sheep have gone astray, Each of
us has turned to his own way; But
the LORD has caused the iniquity
of us all To fall on Him. He was
oppressed and He was afflicted,
Yet He did not open His mouth;
Like a lamb that is led to slaugh-
ter, And like a sheep that is silent
before its shearers, So He did not
open His mouth. By oppression and
judgment He was taken away; And
as for His generation, who considered That He was cut off out of the
land of the living, For the transgression of my people to whom the
stroke was due? His grave was assign-
ed to be with wicked men, Yet a rich
man in His death; Although He had
done no violence, Nor was there any
deceit in His mouth. But the LORD
was pleased To crush Him, putting
Him to grief; If He would render Himself as a guilt offering, He will see His
offspring, He will prolong His days
And the good pleasure of the LORD

will prosper in His hand. As a result
of the anguish of His soul, He will
see it and be satisfied; By His knowledge the Righteous One, My Servant,
will justify the many, As He will
bear their iniquities. Therefore, I
will allot Him a portion with the
great, And He will divide the booty
with the strong; Because He poured
out Himself to death, And was numbered with the transgressors; Yet He
Himself bore the sin of many, And
interceded for the transgressors.

(Isaiah 53:1-12)

Abraham, Isaac, Jacob, Moses, Joseph all looked forward
in faith to God's redemption, which is so graphically described in this chapter.

Many still look forward to the appearance of the Messiah,
and we know that one day He will appear and set all things
in order.

But even in our looking. . .are there perhaps events we
already have overlooked?

If so. . .what bearing do these events have on the final
appearance of the Messiah in righteousness?

And do they have any bearing on our relationship to
God?

And just why do I need a Messiah at all?

Chapter 4

The World's Desperate "Sickness"

The prophet cries:

> **"The heart is more deceitful than all
> else And is desperately sick; Who can
> understand it?. . ."**   (Jeremiah 17:9)

The Spirit of God replies:

> **"I, the LORD, search the heart, I test
> the mind, Even to give to each man
> according to his ways, According to
> the results of his deeds. . . ."**   (Jeremiah 17:10)

Heart disease is the number one killer in North America. The heart is a very vulnerable spot in the human body . . . but the prophet is talking about more than the mechanism in our chests which pumps our blood. He is talking about the very core of our beings, the very seat of our affections and desires.

He is talking about a place so secret that even we do not understand it ourselves; only God does.

However, God has provided a manual, a mirror, whereby we can know what is in our hearts, what our desperate sickness is, and exactly how it may be cured.

The Scriptures are the most exciting book in all the world.

If you have considered them to be just a set of regulations. . ."do this". . ."don't do that". . .you are due for quite a surprise.

> **"No prophecy was ever made by an
> act of human will, but men moved
> by the Holy Spirit spoke from God."**
>
> **(2 Peter 1:21)**

The Bible is not a normal book.

If you consider the phenomena of this book and in particular its portions of prophecy wherein are foretold in minute detail events which have come to pass hundreds of years later, you must conclude that some factor was involved far beyond man's human knowledge.

That factor is the Holy Spirit which is the divine influence of God upon the earth.

If we read the Bible as a historical book or as a book of poetry, we miss its importance, the real meaning.

From the first book of Genesis which records how sin entered into the world, everything in some way is directed to the focal point of all history. Everything in recorded history that precedes this focal point is counted in years forward.

That focal point is the appearance of the Messiah, for He was the fulfillment of God's plan of redemption. He was the only One who could accomplish the task.

In the Garden of Eden, God's Word was challenged by Satan who placed a question mark in Adam's mind. As Adam began to doubt God's Word and commandment, an appetite was created in his human body to partake of something forbidden.

Was it because he was hungry?

No! It was not a natural hunger for food. . .it was a lust for something forbidden.

This is just like human nature today.

We live in a world of laws and restrictions to follow. This is further proof that man is living under sin.

In the Garden of Eden there was only one rule. . . "Don't eat of that one tree." As a result of the direct disobedience of Adam and Eve to this single rule, the basics of life were altered completely.

Basic conditions became bitter. Instead of being able to eat freely of the many varieties of fruits in the Garden of Eden, henceforth Adam would eat his bread "by the sweat of his brow."

No longer would the simple, joyful task of keeping the Garden be his; now he must wrest his living from a ground cursed with thistles and thorns.

Toil became the lot of man, and the pain of giving birth was pronounced on womanhood.

As Adam and Eve allowed the seed of sin to enter into them through doubt, it motivated their physical desires and lodged in their hearts, stirring their emotions.

By the time we come to Genesis 6:5, we read:

> **Then the LORD saw that the wicked-**
> **ness of man was great on the earth,**
> **and that every intent of the thoughts**
> **of his heart was only evil continually.**

SIN GROWS!

Sin grows! It can best be compared to a cancer. . . .It expands in all directions very rapidly. Once it takes hold it becomes embedded. It strangles the natural life processes and paralyzes man's spiritual strength to resist.

Consider once again how it all started:

> **When the woman saw that the tree**
> **was good for food, and that it was**
> **delight to the eyes. . . .**

> **(Genesis 3:6)**

Satan appealed to her imagination. That seed of evil that had been planted now began to take root.

Though Eve had never before eaten of the fruit of that tree, and though she had no ancestors around to tell her it would be delicious. . .she yet saw that it would be good.

She took of the fruit and ate. The serpent didn't make her eat; it was her act, her will. Satan had merely suggested, enticed. The temptation took root in her heart, lodged there, and provoked her to act upon Satan's suggestions.

Satan cannot force a person to sin. He can only suggest and influence, sewing seeds of doubt and rebellion which, if allowed into the heart, bring forth sin.

One writer put it this way:

> **Let no one say when he is tempted,
> "I am being tempted by God"; for
> God cannot be tempted by evil, and
> He Himself does not tempt any one.
> But each one is tempted when he is
> carried away and enticed by his own
> lust. Then when lust has conceived, it
> gives birth to sin; and when sin is ac-
> complished, it brings forth death.**

> **(James 1:13-15)**

Another writer asks the question, "What will a man give in exchange for his soul?"

There was a story recently in our newspapers about a man who paid to have his wife murdered because she refused to give him some money from an inheritance for a business investment.

Throughout the trial, in the face of continuing evidence and testimony, he maintained that he was innocent. All of a sudden he changed his story and confessed that he was guilty.

When the judge asked him what made him change his plea to guilty, he replied, "I suddenly realized that some- where along the line I had lost my soul."

When that realization came to him, the possibility of freedom through pleading innocent had lost all value. He realized he was no longer a man.

SIN'S PROGRESSION

Throughout the Old Testament we may trace the progression of sin in the heart of mankind.

In Genesis 8:21 we read that:

> . . . .the LORD said to Himself, "I
> will never again curse the ground on
> account of man, for the intent of
> man's heart is evil from his youth. . .

In the Psalms, David referred often to the evil of the heart.

> . . .His heart gathers wickedness to
> itself; When he goes outside, he tells
> it.
>
> (Psalm 41:6)
>
> Rescue me, O LORD, from evil men;
> Preserve me from violent men, Who
> devise evil things in their hearts;
> They continually stir up wars.
>
> (Psalm 140:1-2)

David described what he believed to be the ultimate evil in man's heart in these words:

> The fool has said in his heart, "There
> is no God." They are corrupt, they
> have committed abominable deeds;
> There is no one who does good.
>
> (Psalm 14:1)

In the book of Proverbs, Solomon refers to the heart of man more than 75 times, in the book of Ecclesiastes and in the Song of Solomon another 40 times.

Dr. Christiaan Barnard of South Africa has been acclaimed as a great pioneer in the field of heart transplants, but it is God alone who is really able to take a bad heart and make it good.

The prophet Ezekiel proclaimed that there was going to be a different day, a day when the heart of man would be changed and would be evil no more.

> **"And I shall give them one heart,**
> **and shall put a new spirit within them.**
> **And I shall take the heart of stone out**
> **of their flesh and give them a heart of**
> **flesh, that they may walk in My sta-**
> **tutes and keep My ordinances, and do**
> **them. Then they will be My people,**
> **and I shall be their God.**

> **(Ezekiel 11:19-20)**

This same promise is repeated in Ezekiel 36:26-27.

Here is the promise of what would be fulfilled and accomplished in the Messiah:

> **"THIS IS THE COVENANT THAT**
> **I WILL MAKE WITH THEM AFTER**
> **THOSE DAYS, SAYS THE LORD:**
> **I WILL PUT MY LAWS UPON**
> **THEIR HEART, AND UPON THEIR**
> **MIND WILL I WRITE THEM,"**

He then says,

> **"AND THEIR SINS AND THEIR**
> **LAWLESS DEEDS I WILL REMEM-**
> **BER NO MORE."**

> **(Hebrews 10:16-17)**

When sins were once forgiven in the Messiah, they were to be forgiven forever, and forgotten. There would be no need to offer any more sacrifices to blot them out. Man would be enabled to walk right into the very Holy of Holies where God is because of the perfect sacrifice of the Messiah.

This is the fresh, new, life-giving way which the Messiah was to open up by tearing the curtain—His human body— to let us into the holy Presence of God.

Until then, the heart of Adam and of every son and daughter of Adam must fall under the condemnation of the words of Jeremiah:

> **"The heart is more deceitful than all**
> **else And is desperately sick; Who can**
> **understand it?**

> **(Jeremiah 17:9)**

In Messiah we would be able to come to the place that we could pray with David;

> **Search me, O God and know my**
> **heart; Try me and know my an-**
> **xious thoughts; And see if there**
> **be any hurtful way in me, And**
> **lead me in the everlasting way.**

> **(Psalm 139:23-24)**

Satan will and does attempt to influence every human heart. Some, like Eve, put forth their hand to sin at Satan's influence.

Must all?

To be the Messiah, One must parallel the temptations of Adam without the failure of Adam.

To fulfill the requirements of being the Redeemer, He must be tempted in all points like as we are—yet without sin of His own.

Has there ever been such a One?

Is there such a One who has met and successfully overcome this point of temptation as well as all other points involved?

What *are* the other points which must be overcome?

And if there is a Person who meets all the tests, how may we find Him?

We must examine the road signs carefully.

If there is such a Person, we must not. . .we *dare* not . . .miss Him.

Chapter 5

Satan's Greatest Challenge

Sometimes there are many hindrances in our quest for truth. Some hindrances are to be found within our own selves and some are influences outside ourselves. Success or failure often depends on how we react to those outside influences.

A learned man once wrote "The good that I wish, I do not do; but I practice the very evil that I do not wish."

He was putting into words a fact that many another has learned to his own discomfit, that there is something in man, something in each of us, that has at sometime caused us to yield to evil influences when in reality we might not have wished to yield.

Yielding to an outside evil influence is, in a nutshell, what Adam did to lay the foundation for sin, sickness and death in this world and left all mankind vulnerable to the same kind of failure.

The person who jokingly declares "The devil made me do it," is playing with fire. . .for the devil is a very real evil influence.

It was Satan in the person of a serpent who reared his ugly head in Eden and posed the tremendous temptations of that hour to Adam and Eve.

It was influence from the outside that *tempted* man . . .but that which was in his heart is what caused him to *yield*.

Wouldn't any person have acted the same as Adam and Eve?

Is there anyone who would have stood up boldly to the tempter and resisted him?

Is there one who, under the same circumstances, the same temptations, would have remained in true obedience to God?

As Satan influenced and overcame Adam in the Garden of Eden and tore from his grasp the dominion he had over all creation, took from him his sinlessness, and his right to everlasting life. . .it stands to reason as well as to righteous judgment that *in order to get those keys back, there would have to be someone who could overcome Satan in the same arena and under the same circumstances.* Someone must come who could and would be the Redeemer.

If the full consequences of sin were understood by every man and woman, this subject would hold the center of their interest continually, for it is the most important subject in the whole realm of mankind.

For that reason, we need to take a close look at the nature of the temptations which were presented to Adam and which led to his turning his God-given keys of dominion over to the anti-God person of Satan.

The temptations to which Adam was subjected fall into several categories which encompass every area of man's existence. . .physical, spiritual, and emotional.

> **Now the serpent was more crafty than any beast of the field which the LORD God had made. And he said to the woman, "Indeed, has God said, 'You shall not eat from any tree of the garden'?" And the woman said to the serpent, "From the fruit of the trees of the garden we may eat; but from the fruit of the tree which is in the middle of the garden, God has said, 'You shall not eat from it or touch it, lest you die.' " And the serpent**

> said to the woman, "You surely
> shall not die! "For God knows
> that in the day you eat from it
> your eyes will be opened, and
> you will be like God, knowing
> good and evil." When the wo-
> man saw that the tree was good
> for food, and that it was a delight
> to the eyes, and the tree was de-
> sirable to make one wise, she
> took from its fruit and ate; and
> she gave also to her husband
> with her, and he ate.
>   **(Genesis 3:1-6)**

I never cease to be amazed at how simple yet how comprehensive the Bible can be in its presentation of basic truths.

In these six verses we have a study that gets directly to the root of every emotional, spiritual and guilt problem of man.

First and foremost in Satan's attack was his challenge of the Word of God.

This has been his greatest, most successful ploy down through the ages. It worked so well in the Garden of Eden that he has practiced it prodigiously down through the ages ever since.

FIRST ONSLAUGHT

Satan's first cunning onslaught against Eve was the temptation to doubt what God specifically had told her. He struck first at her faith, then at her lustful appetite, and thirdly at her emotions. One led right to the other.

But Satan started with an attack upon the foundation, upon the Word of God!

The initial step to sin in the Garden of Eden taken by our first parents was giving heed to Satan when he disputed God's word.

Today this is still the basis for man rejecting God's master plan of life and trying to direct his own destiny.

It did not work in the Garden of Eden!

It will not work in this 20th century!

Satan knows that the greatest revelation of God to man is God's Word.

If confidence in that Word is undermined, then Satan wins the battle.

We *cannot* know God apart from His word. If that Word is discounted, then there is nothing left.

David said,

> **"If the foundations are destroyed,**
> **What can the righteous do?"**

> (Psalm 11:3)

Wherever you are today, whoever you are, and whatever your place in life, I have *good news* for you! The foundations are still secure! They have not been destroyed. They never *shall* be destroyed for those who will take time to read God's Holy Word and heed His instructions.

Though every demon in hell attack the Word of God, not one promise shall ever fail!

God's message through His prophets to the nation of Israel and later to the whole world was that *what He speaks He will bring to pass*.

In luring Eve, not only did Satan challenge the Word of God, he very slyly added a word which changed the meaning of what God had said entirely.

To Eve, Satan said, "You surely shall *not* die."

But *God* has said:

> **"but from the tree of the knowledge**
> **of good and evil you shall not eat, for**
> **in the day that you eat from it** *you*
> *shall surely die.*"
>
> **(Genesis 2:17)**

After implying doubt as to what God's Word said. . .
and then instilling doubt as to God's goodness in forbid-
ding one of the trees to them. . .Satan used the lust of the
flesh ("saw that the tree was good for food"). . .and the
lust of the eyes ("and that it was a delight on the eyes")
and the pride of life ("the tree was desirable to make one
wise"). . .to effect the temptation which led to the fall of
mankind.

The terrible record became:

> **When the woman saw that the tree**
> **was good for food, and that it was**
> **a delight to the eyes, and that the**
> **tree was desirable to make one wise,**
> *she took from its fruit and ate; and*
> *she gave also to her husband* **with**
> **her, and he ate.**
>
> **(Genesis 3:6)**

DOOR-OPENER

When Eve began to question the Word of God her
troubles began. . .and so did the troubles for all of mankind
thereafter. The doubt formed with the serpent's question
"HAS GOD SAID?" was the *door-opener for all sin of all
mankind of all ages.*

Eve submitted to the desires of her physical body, her
emotions were stirred, and we can see the completed picture of her submission to Satan when her *mind* was challenged.

Notice in Genesis 3:6 the phrase: "she saw that. . .the tree was desirable to make one wise."

The appeal to the intelligence was the final thrust of sin in the life of our first parents.

When we speak of intelligence, as used in this verse, we are not referring to the ability of the brain to add figures, read books, or even the ability of man's mind to create a complicated computer.

Rather, we are speaking of the total corporate being of man.

Many times in the Scriptures this is referred to as man's soul.

It is the very center of his being; it is the development of his attitudes, the type of response he will make to given situations, his personality.

It is his intuition that supersedes his natural reasoning power, for it is this element in a man that makes him know that he is more than flesh and blood.

This is that part of you and me that, if perfected, would make us as God. This is the seed thought planted by Satan in the mind of Eve. This thought caused her to believe that if she ate of the forbidden fruit, she would be *as* God.

Satan said to her: "The reason God doesn't want you to eat of this fruit is because then you would be equal with Him."

Scripture teaches us that the ultimate desire of Satan himself was to be like God, to be equal with God. It was his consuming passion and the reason he became a fallen angel.

> "But you said, in your heart, 'I will
> ascend to heaven; I will raise my
> throne above the stars of God, And
> I will sit on the mount of assembly
> In the recesses of the north. I will

> **ascend above the heights of the
> clouds; I will make myself like
> the Most High.' "**
>
> (Isaiah 14:13-14)

This description of Satan's ambition is sandwiched between Isaiah's report on what that ambition cost him:

> **"How you have fallen from heaven,
> O star of the morning, son of the
> dawn! You have been cut down to
> the earth, You who have weakened
> the nations. . ." "Nevertheless you
> will be thrust down to Sheol, To the
> recesses of the pit."**
>
> (Isaiah 14:12,15)

In tempting Eve, Satan appealed to that same latent ambition for power which also lay within her.

Would Eve like to be as wise as God Himself?

If so, she must doubt His Word, must doubt His good intentions in giving that Word. . .and must act upon her doubt by disobeying that Word.

Figuratively speaking, Eve ate of the "Tree of Doubt" before she reached out her hand and took of the forbidden fruit of the Tree of the Knowledge of Good and Evil.

If Eve, and Adam, at the precise time of their temptation had not let *doubt* enter into their minds. . .what a different story would be told today!

What if Eve had said, "Get behind me, Satan! God told me this and I believe it."?

What if Adam had said, "Satan, it is written!" and had stood steadfast on his very specific instructions from God?

What a difference in the world today! What a difference in circumstances!

Where would be the sin, the sickness, the doubts, the guilts, the broken homes, the wars, the famines, the earthquakes and other disasters we see today?

If only they had not doubted but had stood fast on the "foundations"! Then they would have stood true. . .for the foundations stand true. Today they still stand true and will continue to do so despite repeated attacks by Satan and the self-destructive doubts of man.

As every word that God uttered to Adam and Eve was and is true, so are all the other words of God that have been uttered down through the ages. . .every prophecy. . .every iota.

Wanting truth, we dare not depart from God's words. Wanting truth, we dare not shun a single word or ignore a single guidepost even though *Satan will be at every signpost, in his most clever disguise, speaking his most beguiling language.* . . .

What a weapon we have at our disposal, however, if we hold fast to the unchanging Word of God as handed down to us by the fathers and encompassed by so great a cloud of witnesses. . .

"Satan, it is written. . ."

"IT IS WRITTEN"

It is from the Word of God, through the prophets of God, that we get our absolute guidelines in our search for the Second Adam, the One who can overcome Satan's influence completely, defeat him, and restore to mankind the dominion and life which Satan has usurped.

To find Second Adam, we must adhere strictly to the Scriptures. There is no other guideline, no other absolute.

What did the prophets say?

Isaiah said a Child would be born whose name would be called Wonderful, Counselor, Prince of Peace.

Micah said this birth would take place in Bethlehem. . . .

Daniel said the Messiah would be manifested in the 10th month of the 18th year of Tiberius Caesar. . . .

Signposts.

"It is written."

If God said it, it is true.

MESSIANIC CLAIMS

There have been so many down through the years who have claimed to be the Messiah.

They have attracted followings for a little while. . .and then have vanished from the face of the earth, leaving barely a trace.

So it will be with every false messiah who arises.

Gamaliel, a Jewish doctor of law, had insight into this fact when he spoke these words of the disciples of one who claimed to be the Messiah:

> **"And so in the present case, I say to
> you, stay away from these men and
> let them alone, for if this plan or ac-
> tion should be of men, it will be over-
> thrown; but if it is of God, you will
> not be able to overthrow them; or
> else you may even be found fight-
> ing against God."**
>
> **(Acts 5:38-39)**

If it had not been of God it would have come to naught!

This particular movement did not "come to naught" however, for those whom Gamaliel was discussing were disciples of a Man who appeared on the scene in the Holy Land some 2,000 years ago and claimed to be the Son of God.

His name was Jesus and He lived in Nazareth.

Notice, we said "claimed to be. . . ."

The one thing that made this Man so different from the others who had come was that in no way did He challenge the Word of God. Instead He *insisted* in its authority.

> **"Search the scriptures," He said, "for**
> **in them ye think ye have eternal life:**
> **and they are they which testify of me."**
> **(John 5:39 KJV)**

Do the Scriptures *really* testify of him?

More and more as we have progressed, this man's name has come to mind. . .Jesus of Nazareth. Could it be possible that He is the Second Adam? Does His life fit the criteria of the Scriptures?

The claims of his birth are supernatural. . .the place of his birth coincides wtih the prophecies of Micah. . .the time of his life parallels the time spoken of by Daniel. . . .

We might well class three or four parallels as "coincidence". . .or even five or six. . .but when *many* begin to emerge, we must focus our attention on the parallels which could possibly lead directly, irrevocably and indisputably to the Messiah.

If we begin to examine the possibilities of a man who seemingly fits some of the requirements and he is not what he or his disciples claim, there will come a point of discrepancy which reveals the fraud.

If on the other hand, requirement after requirement is met in parallel after parallel, we must give serious heed to the person who fits this picture.

CLAIMS PROTECTED

When we look at the messianic Scriptures, we see that The Spirit of God was *very protective of the claims of messiahship by making the qualifications very specific.*

In the Bible, truth is absolute. . . .For someone to claim to be the Messiah, *he would have to fulfill every single messianic prophecy to the letter or he would be a false messiah.*

Let us not be afraid to search the Scriptures, but let us approach them boldly.

If the Second Adam has come, we must not miss Him.

If He has not come we must continue our expectancy.

Jesus is One whose life parallels so many of the signposts up to this point that it would be folly to go on calling it coincidence without further and more careful examination.

Suppose that the claims of Jesus are true and that He fits every single guidepost in the Scriptures?

Suppose that He completely parallels the first Adam in every respect. . .in temptations, in dominion, in sonship status, as head of a race, and other points of comparison which will be raised. . .yet is without Adam's failures?

Suppose He meets every criteria of Second Adam?

Would we want to miss the implications of this?

It would mean that Messiah had already come and perhaps our eyes had been holden.

But suppose. . .just suppose. . .there was *one single point* in our parallels of comparison that this One could not meet, one specification that failed.

These implications are also very clear.

But too much is at stake. . .We *must* know!

Chapter 6

A Question of Lineage

Thomas Wolfe, a well-known contemporary writer, recently authored a magazine article in which he referred to this age as "the revival of the me." He stressed that people more than ever are seeking the knowledge of their own identities.

Actually, man has always wanted to know the answers to these vital questions:

"Who am I?"

"Where did I come from?"

"Where am I going?"

"Just what," everyone wants to know, "is my place in the scheme of life?"

Actually, it is God who places this questioning nature within us. . .with the ultimate aim that it will launch us on the search for truth and lead us to the right solutions for our lives.

God Himself posed these questions openly to a runaway servant when He overtook Hagar, Sarai's maid, in the wilderness and inquired of her:

> ". . .where have you come from and
> where are you going?"

> **(Genesis 16:8)**

Man has spent billions of dollars in a search for identity.

Hundreds of best-sellers have dealt with this subject, and the quest has sent millions of people to psychiatrists, psychologists, counselors and religious leaders around the world.

"Who am I?"

The answer could be found for a very few cents in almost any five and ten cents store in the world. Or it could be found free in nearly any library or hotel room anywhere.

For while much of Scripture deals with where man is going, Moses and other early writers under the inspiration of the Spirit of God included enough background to satisfy man's insatiable desire to know who he is if he will only look and see.

It is said that a good writer not only writes so that he can be understood, but that he writes so that he cannot possibly be *mis*understood.

The Spirit of God is the greatest Writer of all time and in the Oracles of God He has laid out in minute detail who we are, where we came from, and where we are going.

While where we came from is a constant factor, who we are and where we are going is a variable directly based upon our present relationship with Jehovah God.

There is only one source book in the world that can tell you where you came from. As a result of this uniqueness, the Bible, God's Holy Word, has come under greater attack by critics than any other publication ever written.

Why?

Because only the Bible provides a definite foundation for the beginnings of man. If its story of creation is not true, then man does not have to accept anything that follows.

If it is true, the rest of the Bible is a guideline to righteousness and reconciliation to God and there are certain conditions that must be met. The eternal rewards of righteousness or unrighteousness are clearly outlined in the Bible.

However it is the Adam nature in man to rebel against righteousness.

There is no limit to man's attempts to stretch his thinking powers to escape the necessity of living a righteous life.

If man can convince himself successfully that the creation story is not valid, then he also can discount the validity of his accountability to an Almighty God.

That is why billions of dollars and countless hours of effort are spent as critics constantly seek to disprove the Genesis account of man's beginnings. That is why there has been such a concerted effort to take consideration of creation out of our classrooms and replace it with evolutionary theories.

But all of their billions and all of their energy and all of their evolutionary teachings cannot nullify one single iota of God's Word.

The foundations have not been destroyed.

They *cannot* be destroyed.

The Genesis account *must* be accepted.

THE SON OF GOD

From the Genesis account, we see that Adam is the son of God by direct creation.

Genesis 1:27 reads, "And God created man (in the Hebrew - Adam) in His own image, in the image of God He created him."

This point of direct sonship comes from Genesis 2:7, "Then the Lord God formed man of dust from the ground, and breathed into his nostrils the breath of life; and man became a living being."

From the creation of Adam and Eve, the first parents, every other person with one exception must be the result of a union between man and woman.

That one exception would be the Messiah who also was to be called the Son of God as Adam was.

As Adam's appearance on this earth was a miracle, the Second Adam also must make a miracle entry upon earth's scene.

According to the prophecy of Genesis 3:15, He was to be the Seed of a woman, and many wonderful things are foretold of Him in the ensuing Scriptures.

Isaiah foretold of a special Child who was to be born in Isaiah 7:14:

> **"Therefore the Lord Himself will**
> **give you a sign: Behold, a maiden**
> **will be with child and bear a son. . ."**
>
> (marginal reading)

In another portion of his prophecy, Isaiah foretells the event in this manner:

> **For a child will be born to us, a son**
> **will be given to us. . .And His name**
> **will be called Wonderful Counselor,**
> **Mighty God, Eternal Father, Prince**
> **of Peace.**
>
> **(Isaiah 9:6)**

Both prophecies are signs on the roadway which began at Genesis 3:15 and lead to that "focal point of history" . . .the actual appearance of the Messiah.

In fact, Isaiah pinpoints this Child even more as a progenitor of David in the following verse:

> **There will be no end to the increase**
> **of His government or of peace, On**
> **the throne of David and over his**
> **kingdom, To establish it and to up-**
> **hold it with justice and righteousness**
> **From then on and forevermore. The**
> **zeal of the LORD of hosts will ac-**
> **complish this.**
>
> **(Isaiah 9:7)**

God had already promised Abraham that in <u>his</u> seed would all the nations of the earth be blessed in such portions of Scripture as Genesis 12:3, 18:18 and 22:18, the latter of which reads;

> **"And in your seed all the nations of**
> **the earth shall be blessed, because**
> **you have obeyed My voice."**

Isaac became heir to the promise in Genesis 26:4:

> **"And I will multiply your descendants**
> **as the stars of heaven, and I will give**
> **your descendants all these lands; and**
> **by your descendants all the nations**
> **of the earth shall be blessed. . . ."**

Following the Highway of the Seed, the next promise was to *Jacob* in Genesis 28:14:

> **"Your descendants shall also be like**
> **the dust of the earth, and you shall**
> **spread out to the west and to the**
> **east and to the north and to the**
> **south; and in you and in your des-**
> **cendants shall all the families of**
> **the earth be blessed."**

Jacob, upon his deathbed, uttered the prophecy which pinpoints *Judah* as the tribe of the Child's coming when by the Holy Spirit he declared:

> **"Judah, your brothers shall praise**
> **you; Your hand shall be on the neck**
> **of your enemies; Your father's sons**
> **shall bow down to you. Judah is a**
> **lion's whelp; From the prey, my**
> **son, you have gone up. He couches,**
> **he lies down as a lion, And as a**
> **lion, who dares rouse him up? The**
> **scepter shall not depart from Judah,**

> Nor the ruler's staff from between his
> feet, Until Shiloh comes, And to him
> shall be the obedience of the peoples.

> (Genesis 49:8-10)

This is re-established years later by the prophecy of Balaam in Numbers 24:17:

> "I see him, but not now; I behold
> him, but not near; A star shall come
> forth from Jacob, And a scepter shall
> rise from Israel. . . ."

Balaam, though disobedient and self-willed in many respects, nevertheless prophesied of the coming Messiah not only in the verse given above, but spoke of His being a King when in fact Israel had no kingly line as yet:

> "He has not observed misfortune in
> Jacob; Nor has He seen trouble in
> Israel; The LORD his God is with
> him, And the shout of a king is
> among them.

> (Numbers 23:21)

However the kingly line had been established by the time that Nathan prophesied to David of his seed:

> "He shall build a house for My name,
> and I will establish the throne of his
> kingdom forever.

> (2 Samuel 7:13)

That this promise went far beyond Solomon is clear since the throne was to be established in the Seed "forever."

Also listen to the Davidic promises of Psalm 89:29 and 36:

> "So I will establish his descendants
> forever, And his throne as the days
> of heaven". . ."His descendants shall

> endure forever, And his throne as
> the sun before Me."

The prophecy of Isaiah 11:1 goes back one generation to David's father with the words of the prophet:

> **THEN a shoot will spring from the
> stem of Jesse, And a branch from
> his roots will bear fruit.**

After further description of the Messiah, Isaiah refers again to the root of Jesse in verse 10.

> **Then it will come about in that day
> That the nations will resort to the
> root of Jesse, Who will stand as a
> signal for the peoples; And His
> resting place will be glorious.**

It is in Isaiah that some of the most graphic and most beautiful of the prophecies concerning the coming Redeemer are to be found. It is hard to choose and select, but let me offer at this point the beautiful words of Isaiah 59:15b-60:3.

> **Now the LORD saw, And it was dis-
> pleasing in His sight that there was
> no justice. And He saw that there was
> no man, And was astonished that there
> was no one to intercede; Then His
> own arm brought salvation to Him;
> And His righteousness upheld Him.
> And He put on righteousness like a
> breastplate, And a helmet of salva-
> tion on His head; And He put on gar-
> ments of vengeance for clothing, And
> wrapped Himself with zeal as a man-
> tle. According to their deeds, so He
> will repay, Wrath to His adversaries,
> recompense to His enemies; To the
> coastlands He will make recom-**

pense. So they will fear the name of
the LORD from the west And His
glory from the rising of the sun, For
He will come like a rushing stream,
Which the wind of the LORD drives.
"And a Redeemer will come to Zion,
And to those who turn from transgression in Jacob," declares the
LORD. "And as for Me, this is My
covenant with them," says the LORD:
"My Spirit which is upon you, and
My words which I have put in your
mouth, shall not depart from your
mouth, nor from the mouth of your
offspring, nor from the mouth of
your offspring's offspring," says the
LORD, "from now and forever."
"ARISE, shine; for your light has
come, and the glory of the LORD
has risen upon you. "For behold,
darkness will cover the earth, And
deep darkness the peoples; But the
LORD will rise upon you, And His
glory will appear upon you. "And
nations will come to your light, And
kings to the brightness of your rising.

This same prophet just a few verses later emphasized
that God had to raise up salvation of His own Self in
the first six verses of the 63rd chapter:

WHO is this who comes from Edom,
With garments of glowing colors
from Bozrah, This One who is majestic in His apparel, Marching in the
greatness of His strength? "It is I
who speak in righteousness, mighty
to save." Why is Your apparel red,

And Your garments like the one
who treads in the wine press? "I
have trodden the wine trough
alone, And from the peoples there
was no man with Me. I also trod
them in My anger, And trampled
them in My wrath; And their life
blood is sprinkled on My garments,
And I stained all my raiment.
"For the day of vengeance was
in My heart, And My year of redemption has come. "And I looked, and
there was no one to help, And I
was astonished and there was no
one to uphold; So My own arm
brought salvation to Me; And My
wrath upheld Me. "And I trod
down the peoples in My anger,
And made them drunk in My
wrath, And I poured out their
lifeblood on the earth."

We have barely lifted a spoonful of drops out of the great sea of messianic prophecies to be found in the Scriptures, but all Scripture converges to express and convince that there must come One who would fit the pattern exactly.

COMPARING LINEAGE

That there was a Man who lived on this earth 2,000 years ago called Jesus of Nazareth is recorded in secular history and many Jewish writings of that day.

That He was born on this earth as a little baby is not in dispute.

However, many special claims about His birth have been made which, if true, would place Him well along the Highway of the Seed.

Nearly 2,000 years ago, a Jewish physician named Luke penned these words which described a remarkable occurrence:

> Now in the sixth month the angel
> Gabriel was sent from God to a city
> in Galilee, called Nazareth, to a vir-
> gin engaged to a man whose name
> was Joseph, of the descendants of
> David; and the virgin's name was
> Mary. And coming in, he said to
> her, "Hail, favored one! The Lord
> is with you." But she was greatly
> troubled at this statement, and
> kept pondering what kind of sal-
> utation this might be. And the
> angel said to her, "Do not be
> afraid, Mary; for you have found
> favor with God. "And behold,
> you will conceive in your womb,
> and bear a son, and you shall
> name Him Jesus. "He will be
> great, and will be called the Son
> of the Most High; and the Lord
> God will give Him the throne of
> His father David; and He will
> reign over the house of Jacob
> forever; and His kingdom will
> have no end." And Mary said
> to the angel, "How can this be,
> since I am a virgin?" And the
> angel answered and said to her,
> "The Holy Spirit will come upon
> you, and the power of the Most
> High will overshadow you; and
> for that reason the holy offspring
> shall be called the Son of God."

(Luke 1:26-35)

Though genealogy is reckoned by fatherhood, the genealogies of the man named Jesus of Nazareth is recorded both by the line of Joseph who wed His mother, Mary, and of Mary herself. These genealogies are recorded by early Jewish writers in Matthew 1:1-16 and in Luke 3:23-38. The lineage in Luke goes back to Adam, the one in Matthew back to Abraham.

Listen to the antecedents listed in Matthew's genealogy of Jesus:

Abraham. . .Isaac. . .Jacob. . .Judah. . .Jesse. . .David. . . and thus on down to another Jacob. . ."and to Jacob was born Joseph the husband of Mary by whom was born Jesus, who is called Christ the Messiah." (verse 16)

In Luke, the line is traced in reverse order to include David. . .Jesse. . .Judah. . .Jacob. . .Isaac. . .Abraham. . . Shem. . .Noah. . .Seth. . .and Adam, the latter designated by the writer as "the son of God." (verse 38)

OTHER COMPARISONS

While we would pause to marvel that both sides of this genealogy are traceable to the many signposts on the Highway of the Seed, we must go on to other points of comparison, for there are many other signs which must be met along the way.

The book in the New Testament called Mark recently was in the world news headlines. It is now an accepted fact that this book was contained in the library of Qumran and portions of it have been identified in the Dead Sea Scrolls.

The opening words of this book are thrilling:

THE beginning of the gospel of Jesus
Messiah, THE SON OF GOD. . .

In the very first chapter of Mark there is another reference to Jesus being the Son of God. This is even greater

than the first, for it is not the opinion of a man, but it is
the very voice of God speaking:

> And it came about in those days
> that Jesus came from Nazareth in
> Galilee, and was baptized by John
> in the Jordan. And immediately
> coming up out of the water, He
> saw the heavens opening, and the
> Spirit like a dove descending upon
> Him; and a voice came out of the
> heavens: "Thou art My beloved Son,
> in Thee I am well-pleased."
>
>   (Mark 1:9-11)

The voice of God speaks again in this same book on
yet another occasion:

> . . .Jesus took with Him Peter and
> James and John, and brought them
> up to a high mountain by them-
> selves. And He was transfigured
> before them; and His garments be-
> came radiant and exceedingly
> white, as no launderer on earth
> can whiten them. And Elijah ap-
> peared to them along with Moses;
> and they were conversing with
> Jesus. And Peter answered and
> said to Jesus, "Rabbi, it is good
> for us to be here; and let us make
> three tabernacles, one for You,
> and one for Moses, and one for
> Elijah." For he did not know what
> to answer; for they became ter-
> rified. Then a cloud formed, over-
> shadowing them, and a voice came

> out of the cloud, "This is My be-
> loved Son, listen to Him!"

(Mark 9:2-7)

DISCIPLES' OPINION

The 12 disciples were the constant companions and followers of Jesus for more than three years. Toward the end of the earthly ministry of Jesus, He asked them this question found in the book of Matthew:

> ". . .Who do people say that the Son of
> Man is?" And they said, "Some say
> John the Baptist; some, Elijah; and
> others, Jeremiah, or one of the
> prophets." He said to them, "But
> who do you say that I am?" And
> Simon Peter answered and said,
> "Thou art the Christ, the Son of
> the living God." And Jesus answer-
> ed and said to him, "Blessed are
> you, Simon Barjona, because flesh
> and blood did not reveal this to you,
> but My Father who is in heaven.

(Matthew 16:13-17)

We have heard the voice of the early prophets such as Isaiah.

We have considered the opinions of His disciples, the early Jewish writers of the New Testament Gospels, and words spoken by God Himself.

Now let us hear a Roman commander, an outsider, so to speak, as he expresses his thoughts on the Sonship of Jesus.

> And when the centurion, who was
> standing right in front of Him, saw

> **the way He breathed His last, he
> said, "Truly this man was the Son
> of God!"**

(Mark 15:39)

Jehovah God has not wanted to leave a shadow of doubt about the One Whom He ordained to be the Messiah. The identity must not be based upon just a single shred of evidence but must rest upon a multitude of facts which cannot be denied.

One of the great benefits of the study of geometry is its use in teaching the ability to reason.

You examine Fact A, add to it Fact B, consider Fact C and so on in orderly sequence.

Suddenly, by fact upon fact, step upon step, you are faced with an unalterable "conclusion."

You cannot reach an absolute conclusion if even one fact fails to gibe with all the others.

As long as all the facts *do* fit together in harmony, we must continue our quest.

Is this indeed the Son of God?

And, if so, where do I fit into the picture?

Chapter 7

Parallels of Temptation

Lineal descent has played a great part in the history of mankind. By it kings and priests have been determined, fortunes have been established or lost, inheritances decided.

The matters we are dealing with here, however, are of such import that even though every lineal base has been touched, we must neglect no other obligation or question in our search.

The natural line of Jesus is traced back to Abraham, Isaac, Jacob, Judah and David through Joseph who married Mary, the mother of Jesus. (Matthew 1)

Through Mary's own line, not only were those descendents listed but the genealogy was taken back through Shem, Noah, and Seth to Adam himself, the description ending with these words, "Adam, the son of God." (Luke 3:38)

Throughout the early chapters of this book, however, we have stressed other requirements and we must not fail to measure our test case by each formula.

According to the prophecy of Daniel 9:25 already cited, the Messiah should have stood revealed on the 10th day of Nisan in the 18th year of Tiberius Caesar.

Oddly enough, by minute figuring, this is the exact day on which Jesus of Nazareth made a triumphal ride into the city of Jerusalem to the loud acclamation of the multitudes.

His appearance coincided *exactly* with the time frame given by Daniel:

**"So you are to know and discern that
from the issuing of a decree to restore**

and rebuild Jerusalem until Messiah
the Prince there will be seven weeks
and sixty-two weeks;

(Daniel 9:25)

But what about the prophesied miracle of birth in Isaiah 7:14?

"Therefore the Lord Himself will
give you a sign: Behold, a maiden
will be with child and bear a son,
and she will call His name Immanuel.
(marginal reading)

Did that marker fit?

And what about the place of his birth as described in Micah 5:2?

"But as for you, Bethlehem Ephrathah,
Too little to be among the clans of
Judah, From you One will go forth
for Me to be ruler in Israel. His go-
ings forth are from long ago, From
the days of eternity."

Could He lay claim to that?

Or did He come from the tribe described in Genesis 49:10?

"The scepter shall not depart from
Judah, Nor the ruler's staff from between his feet, Until Shiloh comes,
And to him shall be the obedience
of the peoples."

So far, not a signpost has failed. Chances for coincidence become more remote with each comparison.

However, there is one test we have stressed which we have not tried.

In discussing the temptations of Adam and Eve and their failures, we have reiterated time and again that Second Adam must absolutely duplicate the conditions of the temptations while at the same time surmounting them.

Was this done?

Tradition and the writers of the New Testament hold to the story that Satan confronted Jesus face-to-face in a historic meeting in a wilderness place during which Jesus suffered three tremendous temptations. They claim that these temptations parallel the temptations of Adam and Eve. . . and that Jesus conclusively won the confrontation.

The story is related in the New Testament by a former Jewish tax gatherer named Matthew who became one of the earliest followers of Jesus:

> **Then Jesus was led up by the Spirit
> into the wilderness to be tempted by
> the devil. And after He had fasted
> forty days and forty nights, He then
> became hungry. And the tempter
> came and said to Him, "If You are
> the Son of God, command that
> these stones become bread." But
> He answered and said, "It is writ-
> ten, 'MAN SHALL NOT LIVE ON
> BREAD ALONE, BUT ON EVERY
> WORD THAT PROCEEDS OUT
> OF THE MOUTH OF GOD.' "
> Then the devil took Him into the
> holy city; and he stood Him on
> the pinnacle of the temple, and
> said to Him, "If You are the Son
> of God throw Yourself down;
> for it is written, 'HE WILL GIVE
> HIS ANGELS CHARGE CON-
> CERNING YOU; And ON THEIR**

> **HANDS THEY WILL BEAR YOU
> UP, LEST YOU STRIKE YOUR
> FOOT AGAINST A STONE.' "**
> **Jesus said to him, "On the other
> hand, it is written, 'YOU SHALL
> NOT TEMPT THE LORD YOUR
> GOD.' " Again, the devil took
> Him to a very high mountain, and
> showed Him all the kingdoms of
> the world, and their glory; and he
> said to Him, "All these things will
> I give You, if You fall down and
> worship me." Then Jesus said to
> him, "Begone, Satan! For it is
> written, 'YOU SHALL WORSHIP
> THE LORD YOUR GOD, AND
> SERVE HIM ONLY,' "** *Then the
> devil left Him; and behold, angels
> came and began to minister to Him.*

(Matthew 4:1-11)

The basic elements of all temptations are clearly described and defined in a unique portion of the New Testament:

> **For all that is in the world, the** *lust*
> *of the flesh* **and the** *lust of the eyes*
> **and the boastful** *pride of life*, **is not
> from the Father, but is from the
> world.**

(I John 2:16)

Notice how all these basics were present in the temptation which took place in the Garden of Eden and which Adam and Eve failed to overcome. . .and how they were present in the temptations of Jesus in which He was more than conqueror!

Compare Genesis 3:6 and the writings of Matthew just quoted:

See the temptations of Satan to

1. Lust of the FLESH:

    to Eve: "Saw that the tree was good for food."

    to Jesus: "Command that these stones become bread."

2. Lust of the EYES:

    to Eve: "It was a delight to the eyes."

    to Jesus: "showed Him all the kingdoms of the world and their glory."

3. PRIDE of Life:

    to Eve: ". . .was desirable to make one wise."

    to Jesus: "Throw Yourself down for it is written 'He will give His angels charge concerning You and on their hands they will bear You up, lest You strike Your foot against a stone."

Now let us compare what happened.

Eve: "She took from its fruit and ate; and she gave also to her husband with her and he ate."

Jesus: "But He answered and said, 'IT IS WRIT-TEN. . . .'"

Now we have not a parallel, but a contrast.

There could be no greater contrast. . .night from day, east from west, north from south, down from up.

Whereas first Adam doubted God's word and failed, the Second Adam stood upon the Word of God as His success-ful weapon and *completely defeated Satan*.

There is another parallel in the temptation we must note and that is that Satan himself used the Word of God. . .or rather his own version of the Word of God. . .to try to further his godless ends.

In tempting Eve, he added to the Word of God and contradicted it. Where God had said they would surely die if they sinned, Satan contradicted this and told them that they would not die.

In tempting Jesus, Satan again used the Word of God, but this time instead of adding to it, he took it out of its context. . .a favorite devil trick. He twisted its meaning!

In quoting from the 91st Psalm to Jesus, Satan said:

> **For He will give His angels charge concerning you, To guard you in all your ways. They will bear you up in their hands, Lest you strike your foot against a stone.**

> ### (Psalm 91:11-12)

If he had not taken this out of context and stopped when he did, Satan would have echoed the prophecy of his own doom which had also been foretold in Genesis 3:15, for the next verse of the Psalm says of the Messiah:

> **You will tread upon the lion and cobra, The young lion and the serpent you will trample down.**

> ### (Psalm 91:13)

What is this but a reaffirmation of the bruising of Satan's head as promised in Genesis 3:15?

Now let us parallel what happened after the temptation:

Angels appeared on the scene both times.

In Eden, an angel was set with flashing sword to guard the way back to the Garden of Eden lest the fallen couple return and eat of the Tree of Life and live forever in their fallen condition.

Angels also appeared after Jesus' ordeal. . .but they were there to minister and to help, not in judgment.

This great story from Matthew has more import than might be seen from casual reading. It would mean much even if we drew the line here, having shown that Second Adam overcame where first Adam failed. . .

But there is so much more to it than that. . .*for both accounts vitally affect the personal life of each and every individual who was ever born on this earth*.

It is a personal walk that each of us has before God, a personal relationship.

We lost our inheritance when first Adam failed, but must it forever be lost?

No! A thousand times, No!

This is a great truth captured graphically by the great Jewish student, Saul of Tarsus, who penned these flaming words:

> **But not as the offence, so also is the free gift. For if through the offence of one [Adam] many be dead, much more the grace of God, and the gift by grace, which is by one man, Jesus Christ, hath abounded unto many.**

> **(Romans 5:15 KJV)**

> **For if by one man's offence death reigned by one; much more they which receive abundance of grace and of the gift of righteousness shall reign in life by one, Jesus Christ.**

> **(Romans 5:17 KJV)**

> **For as by one man's disobedience many were made sinners, so by the**

> obedience of one shall many be
> made righteous.

(Romans 5:19 KJV)

> Therefore as by the offence of one
> judgment came upon all men to
> condemnation; even so by the right-
> eousness of one the free gift came
> upon all men unto justification of
> life.

(Romans 5:18 KJV)

This, then, is the inheritance we have in the Second Adam, the Messiah.

By natural birth we are in Adam. . .like Adam. . ."sinners" by nature, by birth. . . .

. . .But not until Messiah was there a Second Man (a Second Adam) in the likeness of God Who provides the possibility of righteousness for fallen man.

Chapter 8

The Breaking of Bread

A study of the Holy Scriptures is an exciting adventure because we are not dealing with just an ancient manuscript; we are discussing something that is vitally alive. It applies to our lives right now in this 20th century just as it did to the lives of Jewish people 2000, 3000 and 4000 years ago.

Technology and science may change, life styles may change, pace of living may change. . .but the basic spiritual and emotional needs of people have never changed since the day of the man who stands at the head of the human race—the first Adam.

The Word of God tells us that Adam was created in the very image of God. He was created to have communion and fellowship with his Creator, Jehovah God.

For a period of time Adam actually did walk and talk with God in the Garden of Eden until his sin broke that relationship and erected an inpenetrable wall between God and man.

We hear constantly on the news media of walls which exist today. . .the Berlin Wall, the great Wall of China, the political wall called the "Iron Curtain," another called the "Bamboo Curtain."

Many efforts have been made in our time to break down these man-made walls that separate people.

The wall which we are talking about here is more ominous and of far greater importance than any of those listed above because it not only separates one from another but, more importantly, it separates men from the God Who created them.

The story is not all sad, however, for the Bible tells us that the very moment this wall went up between God and

man, God Himself set in motion a plan whereby every man
would be justified to stand before God once again with
that wall completely removed.

This plan is called "REDEMPTION."

What a beautiful word! It is beautiful because of the fulfillment of God's plan of reconciliation between man and
God which it contains.

The final act of tearing down that wall of separation between God and man was consummated in the life, death,
and resurrection of the Messiah. From the very beginning
in the book of Genesis it was declared that one day He
would come to set all men and women absolutely free from
the bondage of sin and death and would bring them back
into the family of God.

CENTRAL THEME

God's plan of redemption to come through the Messiah
became the central theme of every writer of the Old Testament.

Everything recorded in the Holy Bible pointed to the
coming of the Messiah. There is not a book in the Old Testament which does not declare either directly or indirectly
the coming of the sinless One Who could come to take away
the sins of the world.

You could give any number of reasons why the books
of the Old Testament were written.

You could say that they are a history of the Jewish
people. . .and you would be absolutely right.

You could say that they are books of beautiful poetry
. . .and you would be absolutely right.

You could say that they gave the Jewish people a moral
code to live by. . .and you would be right.

You could say that the prophets were the political leaders of their time and kept the nation in line. . .and you would be partially correct.

Most important of all, however, is that the Bible was and is the revelation of the Messiah.

If it were not for this reason, the writings would have fallen far short of their potential.

The purpose of this revelation is the redemption of the Jewish people and all mankind through the Messiah, the Son of God, Who came into the world to suffer the temptations that Adam had suffered, the temptations that you and I suffer. . .but with one important difference: In every temptation He suffered, the Messiah was victorious and overcame the power of Satan by the Word of God.

Only after He had overcome every temptation was He qualified to become the ultimate sacrifice and offering for sin. Through His death He overcame him who had the power of death, the devil. Thus He is able to give the power to become a Son of God, to give eternal life to those who accept it.

In the previous chapter we looked at the temptation of man when, in the Garden of Eden, the serpent challenged God's Word.

God had given a commandment, God spoke. . .but the serpent, Satan, said, "Has God said?"

The moment doubt entered into the minds of Adam and Eve, it opened the door to a flood of temptation that overcame them.

From this story and the parallel experience of the Messiah, we can conclude that if Eve had stopped Satan right at this point and said, "Yes! God has said it and I believe it!" the entire tragic history of mankind which has been written in blood and tears would have been different.

Every evil, every sorrow, every affliction, every disease, and every problem that man suffers today was unleashed at the precise moment when doubt entered into the minds of Adam and Eve.

The second temptation which Adam and Eve experienced, after they began to doubt God's Word, was Satan's appeal to their physical senses and their physical appetites.

In Genesis 3:6:

> **". . .the woman saw that the tree was good for food. . ."**

It was here that she began to imagine in her mind what the fruit of this tree would taste like. The devil was building up his case.

At this point we may ask the question, *"When did sin really enter into the human race?"*

Was it when Adam and Eve took their first bite of the forbidden fruit? Or was it when Eve first was seduced by the arguments of Satan and let these thoughts receive power to rule over her mind?

The consent of our wills, of our bodies, minds, and spirits to the deeds of sin is equivalent in the sight of God to the very commission of sin.

Satan always attacks man with temptation at his weakest points.

Jesus had not eaten for 40 days and the story says that He was very hungry. Satan, realizing the power of the Son of God, asked Him why He did not make bread from stones and satisfy His hunger, His physical appetite.

But Jesus, though hungry, did not yield to the temptation. He responded with the Scriptures.

Remember, Jesus was a rabbi; He knew the Scriptures. Here He used a well-known text from Deuteronomy 8:3.

> "...'MAN SHALL NOT LIVE ON
> BREAD ALONE, BUT ON EVERY
> WORD THAT PROCEEDS OUT
> OF THE MOUTH OF GOD.'"
>
> **(Matthew 4:4)**

The Scriptures often place an emphasis on "bread," a word that has come to be almost synonymous with natural subsistence as a whole. From the beginning it has been considered "the staff of life." Adam's "bread" supply was hard hit by his disobedience. Henceforth, God sentenced him, "By the sweat of your face you shall eat bread."

It would no longer come easy.

When the children of Israel left Egypt under the leadership of Moses, a special bread which we call matzo or unleavened bread had to be prepared without using yeast. The yeast, or the leaven in the bread, represented the element of sin.

Why? Because leaven was something that always expanded and grew. Once a little bit of it got inside, it caused an explosion within the bread which made it rise and expand out of proportion.

This is symbolic of sin as it entered into man in the Garden of Eden.

From that first doubt that led to Adam's first bite in direct defiance of God has sprung every act of immorality and every act of man's inhumanity to man that ever has been conceived.

If we have said it once we have said it hundreds of times: Man's problem is not one of black against white or vice versa, not Jew against Gentile or Polish against Irish. It is not a color war nor an anti-Semitic war.

It is a war of the heart and mind and will of man over that for which he was originally created.

SIGN OF TROUBLE

From Eve's first lustful look at the fruit of that tree, the bread of life has been used by the Old Testament writers to be a sign of trouble.

Even the unleavened bread of the Passover was referred to as the "bread of affliction." Our Jewish ancestors were afflicted for 40 years in the wilderness; but here, as in the Garden, they suffered because they doubted the Word of God. They preferred to believe the word of men before they would believe the Word of Almighty God.

What a parallel we have in the world today when men are willing to gamble their eternal destinies on the theories of frail and changeable men rather than on the eternal Word of an Unchangeable God.

In Psalm 80:5 we read:

> **Thou hast fed them with the bread
> of tears, And Thou hast made them
> to drink tears in large measure.**

What is the Lord trying to say to people today?

The tears we have shed are the result of the basic sin in our lives, and this is separating us from God.

Psalm 127:2 speaks of the "bread of sorrow" in the King James Version and the New American Standard Version puts it this way:

> **It is vain for you to rise up early,
> To retire late, To eat the bread of
> painful labors; For He gives to His
> beloved even in his sleep.**

King Solomon, one of the wisest men who ever lived, spoke of the "bread of wickedness," the "bread of deceit," and the "bread of idleness."

The great prophet Isaiah spoke of the "bread of adversity."

Wherever you look in the Old Testament, the food of life was sorrow.

Though a yearly payment was made to obtain forgiveness of sin, yet there was always that sense of condemnation because redemption was not complete. Something was missing. They had to go back year after year. . . . The sacrifice was never finished!

But there was One Who would come and fulfill the redemption. . .and this is the central theme of the prophets and of every Old Testament writer. Through them God promised one day to send One Who would once and for all take away all the sins of the world.

ONE QUALIFIES

Was there One Who came exactly as they said He would?

Remember the Messiah had to be the completion of every single qualification to the letter or He simply would not be the Messiah.

One day, 2,000 years ago, there was One Who died on a Roman cross and said, "It is finished!"

Those who heard Him say this thought that He was referring to His own life. . .but He was referring to the sacrifice for sin.

"It is finished!"

No more would there have to be another sacrifice for sin, a lamb or animal slain; the complete plan of God for the redemption of mankind was finished!

This same "One," during His lifetime here on earth, one day was discussing the subject of bread with His disciples.

Jesus therefore said to them, "Truly,
truly, I say to you, it is not Moses
who has given you the bread out
of heaven, but it is My Father who
gives you the true bread out of heaven. "For the bread of God is that
which comes down out of heaven,
and gives life to the world."
They said therefore to Him,
"Lord, evermore give us this bread."
Jesus said to them, "I am the bread
of life; he who comes to Me shall not
hunger, and he who believes in Me
shall never thirst. "Truly, truly, I
say to you, he who believes has eternal life. "I am the bread of life. "Your
fathers ate the manna in the wilderness, and they died. "This is the bread
which comes down out of heaven,
so that one may eat of it and not die.
"I am the living bread that came
down out of heaven; if any one eats
of this bread, he shall live forever; and
the bread also which I shall give for the
life of the world is My flesh."

(John 6:32-35, 47-51)

Here is the mystery of all the ages revealed! Here is the
secret to eternal life! Here is the key to receiving the forgiveness of sins and being welcomed back into the family
of God!

It was through our flesh that sin entered into the world.
It was also through one of the basic temptations. . .the lust
of the flesh. Eve doubted, then looked, and then lusted
for that which she was told not to touch.

However, that is not the end of the story.

Another One came, born without sin, Who was placed by God in the same circumstances as the first Adam. However this One did not yield to the temptation but overcame it and thus could say, "I am the Bread of Life."

There is one word I want to emphasize to you in the Scripture quoted above concerning the Messiah as the Bread of Life. The word is "*ANYONE.*"

The Messiah said, ". . .if *any one* eats of this bread, he shall live forever;" and again He said, ". . .he (*any one*) who believes has eternal life."

There has never been another man in Jewish history who could make that statement.

There have been many great men—some prophets, some wise men—but there is only One worthy to be called the MESSIAH.

There is only One Who can give to us eternal life.

This is what redemption is all about.

Chapter 9

When is Sin Sin?

If there had been no sin, there would be no *need* of redemption.

But that need is very real and in finding that need met we must consider one of the most far-reaching questions imaginable and one that poses the need for conclusive answers.

That question is the sin question.

Is there such a thing as absolute sin?

Is it not true that what is sin for one people or one generation may not be sin for another people or another generation?

There are some in the intellectual community of our day who would have the world believe that there is no such thing as absolute sin. It is, they say, only a relative term. Sin is different for every age. It changes with the circumstances. We cannot be definitive.

These arguments appeal to the intellect and convince many who are glad to hear. . .and ready to believe. . . that they have absolutely no responsibility or accountability for their actions.

The argument is often put forth that it is impossible to live without sin or to overcome sin, that no one is, or ever has been, free from the curse of sin.

There are two main problems with this stream of thought:

One, the person of Adam who was created sinless and of whose sinless state we have been given a good description.

Two, the sinlessness of the Second Adam, the Messiah, Who brought redemption to the human race.

Adam's sinless character is established from two directions:

In the first place, he was created by Jehovah God Who was incapable of imperfection. When God said, "Let us make man in our own image," that image was perfection. Perfection means without sin. Also in Genesis 1:31 we read:

> And God saw all that He had made,
> and behold, it was very good. . . .

The entrance of imperfection and sin came through the challenge of Satan to the Word of God.

God hath said, "thou shalt not," and the serpent questioned, ". . .Hath God said?"

God said, "You shall surely die." Satan said, "You surely shall not die."

The transition from the sinless condition to the fallen state of Adam created a great contrast. He left Eden and took with him the sinful nature that thereafter would be a part of everyone born on the face of the earth—with one exception.

There is no better description of the fact of inherited sin than the words of David:

> Behold, I was brought forth in iniquity, And in sin my mother conceived me.
>
> (Psalm 51:5)
>
> All of us like sheep have gone astray. . .
>
> (Isaiah 53:6)
>
> for all have sinned and fall short of the glory of God,
>
> (Romans 3:23)

David also clearly tells the beauties of being released from
the sentence of sin:

> **How blessed is he whose transgres-
> sion is forgiven, Whose sin is cov-
> ered!**

> **(Psalm 32:1)**

Now we have established three things:

One, the original sinless conditions of the first Adam.

Two, the fall of Adam from the sinless condition.

Three, the fact of inherited sin in the life of every person in Adam's race.

IS THIS THE END?

The next question is: "Is this the final condition of man
or did God provide a plan to bring man back into the family of God and provide for the redemption of man from
sin?"

We refer again to that important Scripture in Genesis
3:15 where God speaks to the serpent that deceived Eve:

> **"And I will put enmity Between you
> and the woman, And between your
> seed and her seed; He shall bruise
> you on the head, And you shall
> bruise him on the heel."**

God promised that there would come a Deliverer Who
would strike evil at its head and destroy it once and for all.

*If God created the first Adam sinless, then the Second
Adam Who would redeem the family of man from sin also
would have to be sinless.*

Isaiah gave the first clue as to how this was to be accomplished when he foretold of a special child to be born
who would be called, Immanuel, meaning "God with us."

GOD WITH US!

What a proclamation!

The Spirit of God speaking through the great prophet Isaiah states that *God will walk with man once again upon the earth just as He did in Eden*. However this time, instead of seeing perfect man fall into sin, He will lift man up; He will redeem man from sin and return him to the family of God.

We must look to see if there ever has been One Who could fill this tremendous description completely. Is there One Who has ever walked upon the face of the earth Who could be described as "God with us"?

Has there ever been a Man among men Who could be described as "sinless"?

Paul, an early Jewish scholar, wrote these tremendous words:

> Now all these things are from God,
> who reconciled us to Himself through
> Christ, and gave us the ministry of rec-
> onciliation, namely, that God was in
> Christ reconciling the world to Him-
> self, not counting their trespasses
> against them, and He has commit-
> ted to us the word of reconcilia-
> tion. Therefore, we are ambassadors
> for Christ, as though God were en-
> treating through us; we beg you on
> behalf of Christ, be reconciled to
> God. He made Him who knew no
> sin to be sin on our behalf, that we
> might become the righteousness of
> God in Him.

(2 Corinthians 5:18-21)

Men could fill the greatest libraries of the world with their thoughts and still they could not say more about redemption than the man who had been known as Saul of Tarsus, a disciple of the great rabbi, Gamaliel said in these few words as he wrote under the inspiration of the Holy Spirit.

The simplicity of this gospel establishes that the Messiah had a sinless nature and that God took that nature and poured into it our sins so that in exchange we might receive the goodness and righteousness of God. (I Peter 2:24)

There is a further look at the sinless character of the Messiah and the claims of Jesus in these words:

> Since then we have a great high
> priest who has passed through
> the heavens, Jesus the Son of
> God, let us hold fast our con-
> fession. For we do not have a
> high priest who cannot sym-
> pathize with our weaknesses,
> but one who has been tempt-
> ed in all things as we are, yet
> without sin. Let us therefore
> draw near with confidence to
> the throne of grace, that we
> may receive mercy and may
> find grace to help in time of
> need.

> (Hebrews 4:14-16)

WITHOUT SIN

The Messiah was tempted the same as we are, as the first Adam was; yet He never gave way to that temptation or sinned; therefore, we can conclude once again from this verse that the Messiah was without sin.

The sinless nature of the Messiah was one of His most important characteristics because without it He would not have qualified to bear our sins. He had to take upon Himself something which He did not possess. Otherwise He would have been sacrificed for His own sins and could not have been the Substitute for ours. He was a High Priest Who was without sin!

Peter also gives us a description of the sinless condition of the Messiah:

> **For you have been called for this purpose, since Christ also suffered for you, leaving you an example for you to follow in His steps, WHO COMMITTED NO SIN, NOR WAS ANY DECEIT FOUND IN HIS MOUTH; and while being reviled, He did not revile in return; while suffering, He uttered no threats, but kept entrusting Himself to Him who judges righteously; and He Himself bore our sins in His body on the cross, that we might die to sin and live to righteousness; for by His wounds you were healed. For you were continually straying like sheep, but now you have returned to the Shepherd and Guardian of your souls.**

> **(I Peter 2:21-25)**

The Messiah never sinned. Therefore that means that through the sacrifice for sin that the Messiah made, we now have the possibility of returning to fellowship with God in this life.

It is not an automatic process.

There is a beginning action required on our part. . . .
We have to do something, but this is not complicated.

It does not require long and tedious study or stained
glass windows or a beautifully robed man at an altar.

It does not require what the world thinks of as a con-
version from one religion to another, from one weakness to
the failures of another system of religion.

God has already created the necessary altar. . .right in
our hearts, in the most inner being of our nature. . . .It is
there and waiting to be stirred up. All we need do is—
RECEIVE!

Those who recognize and receive the Messiah into their
hearts and lives have the forgiveness of their sins.

This is the plan of the ages. It is the plan of redemption.
It is the one and only way through which we can be reconciled to God. It is just that simple. . . .

As Paul said, "We beg you on behalf of Messiah, BE
RECONCILED TO GOD."

Paul, through a careful study of the Scriptures and close
scrutiny of the claims made by the disciples of Jesus of
Nazareth, had come to the unshakeable conclusion that
Jesus was the Messiah. It was of Him that he penned these
words in the New Testament:

> **And not only this, but we also exult
> in God through our Lord Jesus Christ,
> through whom we have now received
> the reconciliation. Therefore, just as
> through one man sin entered into the
> world, and death through sin, and so
> death spread to all men, because all
> sinned—But the free gift is not like the
> transgression. For if by the transgres-**

> sion of the one the many died, much
> more did the grace of God and the
> gift by the grace of the one Man,
> Jesus Christ, abound to the many.

(Romans 5:11, 12 & 15)

THE THIRD PARALLEL

That brings us to a precious third parallel. . .ourselves.

By believing in and accepting the true Messiah, we are made "partakers of the divine nature." (II Peter 1:4) Even we become "without sin."

As Adam was without sin before his disobedience. . . so we may become cleansed and without sin before God simply by heart belief in the atoning work of Him Who knew no sin but was willing to become sin for us.

> If we confess our sins, He is faithful
> and righteous to forgive us our sins
> and to cleanse us from all unright-
> eousness.

(I John 1:9)

One of the great curses of the ages has been the guilt which has lain heavily upon the hearts and souls of men and women.

The question of sin *must* be dealt with. . .but psychiatrists, psychologists, educators, and. . .yes, even many ministers and rabbis. . .have sought ways to alleviate the load of that guilt without much success.

Only through the sinless Messiah can we find a successful solution. It comes only as a result of getting rid of the thing that causes our guilt: sin.

In the sight of men we never will be perfect, but thank God for what the Messiah is able to do for us through our belief in and acceptance of Him.

As one studies the prophecies of the Old Testament, as one scrutinizes the claims of the man Jesus, as one hears the reports of those who have come to believe that this might truly be the One without sin, one is led to further examination:

Was the man Jesus truly sinless?

And did He, *could* He, meet the other criteria necessary to establish the conclusive identity of the Second Adam?

Chapter 10

Love's Sacrifice

It was not just for preparing this book that the word "parallels" has consistently come to my mind over the years. I long have had a saying that "All truth is parallel." This applies in every walk of life.

Also I long have realized and used countless parallels in the Scriptures as they apply unmistakably to the Messiah.

However, I never realized until I was deep into the preparation of this book how very many parallels of the Messiah reach all the way back to where we started. . .to the Garden of Eden.

We go back there now to pursue another parallel that must be completely fulfilled before claim to messiahship can be validated. . .the parallel of the sacrifice.

With Adam's alienation from God and his inability to cover his own nakedness by fashioning cover from fig leaves, God Himself instituted. . .and executed. . .the first blood sacrifice for the atonement for sin when He slew an animal to make clothes of skin for the errant couple.

After this the shedding of animal blood as the atonement for sin was instituted.

The writer of Hebrews referred to this years later with this significant statement:

> . . .without shedding of blood there
> is no forgiveness.
>
> (Hebrews 9:22)

It was on this point that Cain thought he had a "better way." He would devise his own salvation. He would come up with something prettier or more dignified.

Just what he was trying to accomplish. . .and what he failed to accomplish. . .was delineated in point after point in an earlier chapter.

Cain brought an offering of the fruit of the ground instead of the approved offering, a firstling from the flock. He was even given another opportunity to comply with God's requirements, but spurned repentance and continued his willful way.

He chose to bring an offering from the ground which was under God's judgment and condemnation. His act denied that sin had separated him from God or that he needed to be reconciled to God. His act denied his need for the death of a substitute.

Abel's offering on the other hand, a slain lamb, pointed to redemption through the blood of a lamb. This need for sacrifice was taught him by his parents and was passed on down through the ages. It proclaimed trust in the grace of God which provided atonement through the blood of the lamb. . .and looked forward to One Who was to come Who would fulfill all the obligations of such a sacrifice.

In the Books of Moses we read about the various sacrifices and offerings required in approaching God. They each sufficed within the limits imposed by God but there always existed that need to sacrifice again and again and again.

It didn't last.

It must be repeated with appropriate ceremony at intervals and locations specified by God.

However each offering spoke in some way of the one great Sacrifice to come Who would fulfill all of the conditions and Whose efficacy would endure to all generations.

The Passover lamb not only spoke of a place of safety for the firstborn of Israel when the death angel passed through Egypt. . .it forespoke of the complete covering for sin that was to be provided in the one perfect Sacrifice Who would shield against future judgment.

The scapegoat spoke of One to come upon Whom we vicariously might lay all of our sins and transgressions.

Many of the sacrifices and ceremonies have been mystical in scope, but once in a while there has appeared among the writings of the prophets such a clear, lucid explanation of what the sacrifice was all about it would seem that every eye on earth would see it and understand.

Read what Isaiah said in one of the most powerful portions of Scripture ever recorded:

> **Who hath believed our report? and
> to whom is the arm of the LORD re-
> vealed? For he shall grow up before
> him as a tender plant, and as a root
> out of a dry ground: he hath no form
> nor comeliness; and when we shall
> see him, there is no beauty that we
> should desire him. He is despised and
> rejected of men; a man of sorrows,
> and acquainted with grief: and we
> hid as it were our faces from him;
> he was despised, and we esteemed
> him not. Surely he hath borne our
> griefs, and carried our sorrows: yet
> we did esteem him stricken, smitten
> of God, and afflicted. But he was
> wounded for our transgressions, he
> was bruised for our iniquities: the
> chastisement of our peace was upon
> him; and with his stripes we are heal-
> ed. All we like sheep have gone as-
> tray; we have turned every one to
> his own way; and the LORD hath
> laid on him the iniquity of us all.**

**He was oppressed, and he was af-
flicted, yet he opened not his mouth:
he is brought as a lamb to the slaugh-
ter, and as a sheep before her shearers
is dumb, so he openeth not his mouth.
He was taken from prison and from
judgment: and who shall declare his
generation? for he was cut off out of
the land of the living: for the transgression of my people was he stricken.
And he made his grave with the wicked,
and with the rich in his death; because
he had done no violence, neither was
any deceit in his mouth. Yet it pleased
the LORD to bruise him; he hath put
him to grief: when thou shalt make
his soul an offering for sin, he shall
see his seed, he shall prolong his days,
and the pleasure of the LORD shall
prosper in his hand. He shall see of
the travail of his soul, and shall be
satisfied: by his knowledge shall my
righteous servant justify many; for
he shall bear their iniquities. Therefore will I divide him a portion with
the great, and he shall divide the spoil
with the strong; because he hath poured out his soul unto death: and he was
numbered with the transgressors;
and he bear the sin of many, and made
intercession for the transgressors.**

(Isaiah 53:1-12 KJV)

Isaiah was speaking of a Sacrifice, but this Sacrifice was
to be a Person.

That Person must be pure, spotless, without blemish,
without sin.

The One Who existed supernaturally before the creation, the One who experienced a supernatural birth into this world, the One who was tempted in every point as a human and yet refused to yield to temptation and remained without sin. . .would He not qualify to be this Sacrifice?

Almost every school child can quote the 23rd Psalm from memory, and it is a beautiful Psalm. However, right next to it is one of the most significant messianic Psalms ever to flow from King David's pen.

Highly prophetically, portions of it read like this:

> My God, my God, why hast thou forsaken me? why art thou so far from helping me, and from the words of my roaring?. . .But I am a worm, and no man; a reproach of men, and despised of the people. . .All they that see me laugh me to scorn; they shoot out the lip, they shake the head, saying, He trusted on the LORD that he would deliver him: let him deliver him, seeing he delighted in him. . .Many bulls have compassed me: strong bulls of Bashan have beset me round. They gaped upon me with their mouths, as a ravening and a roaring lion. I am poured out like water, and all my bones are out of joint: my heart is like wax; it is melted in the midst of my bowels. My strength is dried up like a potsherd; and my tongue cleaveth to my jaws; and thou hast brought me into the dust of death. For dogs have compassed me: the assembly of the wicked have inclosed me: they pierced my hands and my feet. I may tell all my bones: they

> look and stare upon me. They part my
> garments among them, and cast lots
> upon my vesture.

> (Psalm 22:1, 6-8, 12-18 KJV)

We have paralleled Jesus' background with many prophecies as to the time and manner of the appearance of Messiah.

We have paralleled his experience in confrontation with Satan with that of first Adam.

Now may we dare to measure his death against the requirements for the blood sacrifice and the prophecies of the Messiah in such Scriptures as those quoted above?

Jesus had this to say about His own death:

> "For this reason the Father loves Me,
> because I lay down My life that I may
> take it again. No one has taken it
> away from Me, but I lay it down on
> My own initiative. I have authority to
> lay it down, and I have authority to
> take it up again. This commandment
> I received from My Father."

> (John 10:17-18)

Shortly before the arrest and death of Jesus, Caiaphas, the high priest, who was not a disciple of Jesus, was moved upon to prophesy and spoke these telling words:

> But a certain one of them, Caiaphas,
> who was high priest that year, said
> to them, "You know nothing at all,
> nor do you take into account that it
> is expedient for you that one man
> should die for the people, and that
> the whole nation should not perish."
> Now this he did not say on his own
> initiative; but being high priest that

> year, he prophesied that Jesus was
> going to die for the nation; and not
> for the nation only, but that He
> might also gather together into one
> the children of God who are scat-
> tered abroad.

> (John 11:49-52)

The full story of the sacrifice of Jesus is told in the first four books of the New Testament: Matthew, Mark, Luke and John.

The death Jesus died on the cross fulfilled many of the prophecies spoken concerning the Messiah.

Even the way He arrived in Jerusalem for that event is significant:

> And the disciples went and did just
> as Jesus had directed them, and
> brought the donkey and the colt,
> and laid on them their garments, on
> which He sat.

> (Matthew 21:6-7)

> Rejoice greatly, O daughter of Zion!
> Shout in triumph, O daughter of Je-
> rusalem! Behold, your king is com-
> ing to you; He is just and endowed
> with salvation, Humble, and mount-
> ed on a donkey, Even on a colt, the
> foal of a donkey.

> (Zechariah 9:9)

The manner of His betrayal by a companion is a fulfill-ment of Scripture.

> Now he who was betraying Him gave
> them a sign, saying, "Whomever I
> shall kiss, He is the one; seize Him."

> And immediately he came to Jesus
> and said, "Hail, Rabbi!" and kissed
> Him.
>
> (Matthew 26:48-49)
>
> Even my close friend, in whom I trust-
> ed, Who ate my bread, Has lifted up
> his heel against me.
>
> (Psalm 41:9)

Let's look and compare the crucifixion point upon point
in the 22nd Psalm and related Scriptures:

Jesus' cry upon the cross was:

> **"ELI, ELI, LAMA SABACHTHANI?"**
> that is, **"MY GOD, MY GOD, WHY
> HAST THOU FORSAKEN ME?"**
>
> (Matthew 27:46)
>
> MY God, my God, why hast Thou
> forsaken me?
>
> (Psalm 22:1)

Look at His reproach:

> Then they spat in His face and beat
> Him with their fists, and others slap-
> ped Him.
>
> (Matthew 26:67)
>
> In the same way the chief priests,
> along with the scribes and elders,
> were mocking Him, and saying,
> "He saved others; He cannot save
> Himself. He is the King of Israel; let
> Him now come down from the cross,
> and we shall believe in Him. "HE
> TRUSTS IN GOD; LET HIM DE-
> LIVER Him now, IF HE TAKES

> **PLEASURE IN HIM; for He said,
> 'I am the Son of God.' "**
>
> (Matthew 27:41-43)

> But I am a worm, and not a man, A
> reproach of men, and despised by
> the people. All who see me sneer at
> me; They separate with the lip, they
> wag the head, saying, "Commit thy-
> self to the LORD; let Him deliver him;
> Let Him rescue him, because He de-
> lights in him."
>
> (Psalm 22:6-8)

History tells us that in the act of crucifixion, the cross
was dropped into the hole with such force that the victim's
joints were torn out of place. Compare:

> I am poured out like water, And all
> my bones are out of joint; My heart
> is like wax; It is melted within me.
>
> (Psalm 22:14)

Also compare that with what happened when Jesus' side
was pierced:

> but one of the soldiers pierced His
> side with a spear, and immediately
> there came out blood and water.
>
> (John 19:34)

The dry mouth, tongue cleaving to the mouth, was another known effect of crucifixion:

> My strength is dried up like a pot-
> sherd, And my tongue cleaves to
> my jaws; and Thou dost lay me
> in the dust of death.
>
> (Psalm 22:15)

When He asked for a drink to alleviate His thirst, look at what transpired:

> **THEY GAVE HIM WINE TO DRINK MINGLED WITH GALL;** and after tasting it, He was unwilling to drink.
>
> (Matthew 27:34)

> They also gave me gall for my food, And for my thirst they gave me vinegar to drink.
>
> (Psalm 69:21)

His hands and feet were pierced.

> And when they came to the place called the Skull, there they crucified Him and the criminals, one on the right and the other on the left.
>
> (Luke 23:33)

> For dogs have surrounded me; A band of evildoers has encompassed me; They pierced my hands and my feet.
>
> (Psalm 22:16)

Here's what happened about His garments:

> And when they had crucified Him, **THEY DIVIDED UP HIS GARMENTS AMONG THEMSELVES, CASTING LOTS;**
>
> (Matthew 27:35)

> They divide my garments among them, And for my clothing they cast lots.
>
> (Psalm 22:18)

Traditionally, bones were broken to hasten the death of crucifixion victims. However, according to God's Word, no sacrifice was to have its bones broken.

> . . ."nor are you to break any bone
> of it. . ."
>
> **(Exodus 12:46)**

How remarkable, then, these verses:

> **The soldiers therefore came, and broke
> the legs of the first man, and of the
> other man who was crucified with
> Him; but coming to Jesus, when they
> saw that He was already dead, they
> did not break His legs;**
>
> **(John 19:32-33)**

> **He keeps all his bones; Not one of
> them is broken.**
>
> **(Psalm 34:20)**

The fact that He was "reckoned with transgressors" is told in these words:

> **And when they came to the place
> called The Skull, there they cruci-
> fied Him and the criminals, one on
> the right and the other on the left.**
>
> **(Luke 23:33)**

> **Therefore, I will allot Him a portion
> with the great, And He will divide
> the booty with the strong; Because
> He poured out Himself to death,**

> And was numbered with the trans-
> gressors; Yet He Himself bore the
> sin of many, And interceded for
> the transgressors.
>
> (Isaiah 53:12)

His final words were these:

> And Jesus, crying out with a loud
> voice, said, "Father, INTO THY
> HANDS I COMMIT MY SPIRIT."
> And having said this, He breathed
> His last.
>
> (Luke 23:46)

> Into Thy hand I commit my
> spirit;
>
> (Psalm 31:5a)

So many points of comparison and yet we still have just glossed over!

Yet even with the few points covered, we see that Jesus has become the exact photographic Image foretold by the prophets many years before. . .the perfect Sacrifice Who was to come and Who did come.

It must have been a careful weighing of such prophecies that led John the Baptist, another Jew, to his convictions when he stood at the shore of the Sea of Galilee 2,000 years ago and made his beautifully simple pronouncement to his disciples as he pointed to Jesus:

> . . ."Behold, the Lamb of God who
> takes away the sin of the world!"
>
> (John 1:29)

If such a pronouncement is true. . .surely we must not miss it.

If this is God's chosen Sacrifice, must we, like Cain, seek to substitute another?

Could this indeed be the Second Adam? The Messiah!

If He is not, surely close examination will reveal the discrepancies.

And if He is, surely the parallels to be drawn with the first Adam will hold up under the closest scrutiny.

A PERSONAL QUESTION

But now a personal question arises: What does God want from me? What sacrifice can I make?

God does not require a sacrifice from you!

God knew that man could not even keep the law. Therefore in His love. . .not willing that man should have to stay in his sins and under the guilt of his sinful acts. . .God provided a perfect redemption, one that we could point to without condemnation:

> **"For God so loved the world, that He
> gave His only begotten Son, that who-
> ever believes in Him should not perish,
> but have eternal life."**
>
> **(John 3:16)**

He came 2,000 years ago just as the prophets said He would, qualified in every point. Tempted in all points like Adam and Eve, tempted in all points such as you and I, yet He was without sin. He lived a sinless life so that He might die as the sacrificial Lamb, the perfect Sacrifice.

No doubt Satan felt great glee as he watched Adam and Eve succumb to his temptations.

Satan at the time well may have said, "It is finished," referring to God's perfect creation and to the communion between God and man.

"It is finished. They are separated forever."

But that wasn't the end of the story.

The real "finish," the final argument to sin and separation, occurred on a cross 2,000 years ago when it was the
Messiah Who exclaimed, "It is finished!"

It was only then that the "author and perfecter (or
'finisher') of faith" made a final provision for man.

Evil entered into humanity in the Garden, but it is redemption that is completed and perfected in Messiah Jesus.

> . . .where sin increased, grace abounded
> all the more,

> > **(Romans 5:20)**

Destruction began in the Garden:

> **"The thief comes only to steal, and
> kill, and destroy. . .**

> > **(John 10:10)**

But Satan's destruction itself was destroyed when the
Righteous One was come:

> **. . .The Son of God appeared for this
> purpose, that He might destroy the
> works of the devil.**

> > **(I John 3:8)**

Chapter 11

Dominion Reclaimed

To qualify conclusively as the Messiah, one would have to return to us *every single thing* we lost when Adam rebelled against God. A slipshod comparison will not suffice. He must meet the demands head-on, point on point, without compromise and without apology.

Not only must our sonship and our sinless nature be restored through the work of the Messiah, but other qualities which were lost must be placed within our grasp.

What about God-given power, our authority, our dominion? Surely God created man a little lower than the angels and placed him in a position of authority and dominion!

Of Adam's authority, we read:

> **And God blessed them; and God said
> to them, "Be fruitful and multiply,
> and fill the earth, and subdue it; and
> rule over the fish of the sea and over
> the birds of the sky, and over every
> living thing that moves on the earth."
> Then God said, "Behold, I have given
> you every plant yielding seed that is
> on the surface of all the earth, and
> every tree which has fruit yielding
> seed; it shall be food for you;**
>
> (Genesis 1:28-29)

Adam's dominion of the earth is confirmed in these words:

> **And out of the ground the LORD
> God formed every beast of the field
> and every bird of the sky, and
> brought them to the man to see**

> what he would call them; and what-
> ever the man called a living creature,
> that was its name.
>
> (Genesis 2:19)

God placed everything that He had created upon the earth under the power and authority of Adam with the exception of one single tree which was called the Tree of Conscience.

Once Adam ate of the fruit of this tree, he would be aware of right and wrong, of good and bad. The sentence was "If you eat of its fruit, you will be doomed to die."

He ate. . .and every man after him inherited the curse that resulted from this one act of sin.

I have heard this referred to as "one *small* act of sin."

It was never small.

This one sin was the costliest, blackest, worst act ever committed, for it opened upon a perfect creation all the heartache, sickness, suffering and death which has ever come.

In the beginning Adam was given all authority. He was given dominion over all of nature. *Everything* was subject to him, but with the entrance of sin, all of that power and authority was lost and he became instead the servant and slave of the soil.

> Then to Adam He (God) said, "Be-
> cause you have listened to the voice
> of your wife, and have eaten from
> the tree about which I commanded
> you, saying, 'You shall not eat from
> it'; Cursed is the ground because of
> you; In toil you shall eat of it All
> the days of your life. Both thorns
> and thistles it shall grow for you;

> **And you shall eat the plants of the
> field; By the sweat of your face
> You shall eat bread, Till you re-
> turn to the ground, Because from
> it you were taken; For you are
> dust, And to dust you shall re-
> turn."**
>
> **(Genesis 3:17-19)**

I don't think we have ever realized what a truly terrible transaction took place when Adam put forth his hand to sin.

Casual references to Adam and Eve and the apple and the serpent abound, often jestingly, in advertising, in songs, in everyday conversation, on bumper stickers. . .but we *have never really understood the depth, the profundity, of what actually transpired as a result of that one act of disobedience.*

God had placed man in a perfect setting, had given him companionship and plenty, had created for him a veritable paradise. . .and had handed him the keys of dominion over this entire creation.

Not only that, but he held the keys to eternal life. Without sin, man would never have had to die.

Adam in his one act of disobedience took these God-given keys and counted them nothing!

In that one act, he actually *abdicated* his command.

He actually took the keys of dominion and power that God had given to him and *willfully turned them over to Satan.*

By his act, he placed himself and all his progeny under the dominion and power of Satan.

He placed man under the dominion of death.

What bondage, what subservience, he placed entire mankind under!

No wonder it would take Another sent from God, a Messiah to undo the bonds, to break the yokes, to snatch the keys of dominion back from Satan and restore them to the rightful hands of mankind.

What Person could do this?

Paul declared the power, authority and dominion of the Messiah in I Corinthians 15:24-27:

> "then comes the end, when He delivers up the kingdom to the God and Father, when He has abolished all rule and all authority and power. For He must reign until He has put all His enemies under His feet. The last enemy that will be abolished is death. For HE HAS PUT ALL THINGS IN SUBJECTION UNDER HIS FEET..."

Paul had a strong grasp on the issues, on what must be accomplished by the Messiah. No wonder he sought to measure any claimants to the messiahship by these characteristics.

No doubt he carefully weighed such words as these written by the tax collector Matthew:

> The result was that when Jesus had finished these words, the multitudes were amazed at His teaching; for He was teaching them as one having authority, and not as their scribes.

(Matthew 7:28-29)

He must also have heard the report of a learned physician named Luke who recorded these words:

> But passing through their midst, He
> went His way. And He came down
> to Capernaum, a city of Galilee.
> And He was teaching them on Sab-
> bath days; and they were continu-
> ally amazed at His teaching, for His
> message was with authority. And
> there was a man in the synagogue
> possessed by the spirit of an un-
> clean demon, and he cried out
> with a loud voice, "Ha! What do
> we have to do with You, Jesus of
> Nazareth? Have You come to des-
> troy us? I know who You are - the
> Holy One of God!" And Jesus re-
> buked him, saying, "Be quiet and
> come out of him!" And when the
> demon had thrown him down in
> their midst, he went out of him
> without doing him any harm. And
> amazement came upon them all,
> and they began discussing with one
> another, and saying, "What is this
> message? For with authority and
> power He commands the unclean
> spirits, and they came out."

> (Luke 4:30-36)

Jesus Himself spoke of the ultimate power He claimed had been given to Him by Jehovah God, which is the power over death:

> "For this reason the Father loves
> Me, because I lay down My life that
> I may take it again. No one has

> taken it away from Me, but I lay
> it down on My own initiative. I have
> authority to lay it down, and I have
> authority to take it up again. This
> commandment I received from My
> Father."
>
> (John 10:17-18)

> . . .Jesus came up and spoke to them,
> saying, "All authority has been given
> to Me in heaven and on earth.
>
> (Matthew 28:18)

Jesus' claim was that no person, neither Roman nor Jew, took His life from Him, but that He willingly and obediently gave it to accomplish a purpose. . .that at His own will and according to His own ability, He took His life back up again to establish once and forever His dominion over death.

Could this, many wondered, be the fulfillment of the prophecy in Isaiah:

> He will swallow up death for all time,
> And the LORD God will wipe tears
> away from all faces, and He will re-
> move the reproach of His people
> from all the earth; For the LORD
> has spoken. And it will be said in
> that day, "Behold, this is our God
> for whom we have waited that He
> might save us. This is the LORD for
> whom we have waited; Let us rejoice
> and be glad in His salvation."
>
> (Isaiah 25:8-9)

The first Adam gave away dominion and brought death. The Second Adam will restore dominion and bring life. The Bible and secular history as well are full of evidence that there is only one Person in all of history Who can rightfully claim that title.

We must be sure!

Upon Him depends our very beings:

Who we are now. . .

Where we are now. . .

What we *have* now. . .

And what we could be and what we could have. . .in Him.

We must know!

What was His absolute final purpose? And how well did He fulfill that?

Chapter 12

One Final Foe

> **PRAISE THE LORD! For it is good
> to sing praises to our God; For it is
> pleasant and praise is becoming. The
> Lord builds up Jerusalem; He gathers
> the outcasts of Israel. He heals the
> broken-hearted, And binds up their
> wounds.**
>
> (Psalm 147:1-3)

It is in the spirit of praise that we begin this chapter of our Adam and Messiah parallels. . .and with good reason.

From the book of the great Jewish prophet Isaiah, we read:

> And on this mountain He will swal-
> low up the covering which is over
> all peoples, Even the veil which is
> stretched over all nations, He will
> swallow up death for all time, And
> the Lord God will wipe tears away
> from all faces, And He will remove
> the reproach of His people from all
> the earth; For the Lord has spoken.
> And it will be said in that day, "Be-
> hold, this is our God for whom we
> have waited that He might save us.
> This is the LORD for whom we have
> waited; Let us rejoice and be glad in
> His salvation."
>
> (Isaiah 25:7-9)

The ultimate truth that always emerges in God's Word is that regardless of how we look at the Scriptures, the predominant theme is God's "Plan of Redemption."

God's "Plan of Redemption" is the method which the Lord God used to bring man back into fellowship with Himself after the separation of sin ended in death, not only to Adam and Eve, but also to us as their descendants, for sin became an inherent part of all our spiritual beings.

God had said that in the day that they ate of the Tree of the Knowledge of Good and Evil, they would surely die.

They ate. . .and they died. . .but we must ask "What kind of death was it?"

Death became the ruling factor in their beings and eventually it conquered Adam and Eve and they died, as we do today, a natural death.

From the time Adam and Eve were chased out of the Garden of Eden until this very moment, a constant battle has been waged against the elements and the forces of nature.

Man has unleased the power of the atom; he has walked upon the face of the moon; he has developed computers that expand and multiply his knowledge millions of times, but. . .*he has not conquered death.*

But one Man did!

THAT ONE MAN!

That one Man is the secret theme of the entire revelation of God to man through that which is known as the Holy Bible.

From the book of Genesis we read the continuing story of His work, His personality, and His mission. That Man is the Messiah Whom God promised to send not only to re-

deem His people Israel, the Jewish people, but also to save
the multitudes of the Gentiles.

> **The people who walk in darkness**
> **Will see a great light; Those who**
> **live in a dark land, The light will**
> **shine on them.**
>
> **(Isaiah 9:2)**

Beginning with the beginning, throughout the Tenach
the subject of every story from the allegorical lives and experiences of the patriarchs to the warning messages of the
prophets, in some way points to the Anointed One Who
would one day overcome the power of death.

Three hundred and thirty-three times in the Tenach
there is a direct reference to, or description of, this Messiah,
this Man sent from God to redeem His people. Every event
in the experience of the Jewish people in some way was
leading up to the appearance of the Anointed One Whom
God said He would send to take away the sin of the world
. . .and with sin, death.

In all of the experiences of man, there is no greater contrast than that between life and death. Death and life are
absolute opposites, more opposite even than light and darkness.

They represent the greatest contrast of human knowledge because life is the genesis, the beginning spark of life,
and death seems to be the dispersion of the sparks, the
nemesis, the destruction.

WHAT DOES THIS MEAN?

> **For since by a man came death, by**
> **a man also came the resurrection of**
> **the dead. For as in Adam all die, so**
> **also in Christ all shall be made alive.**
>
> **(I Corinthians 15:21-22)**

Death came because of what Adam did; but eternal life came because of what the Messiah, Jesus, did.

What did Adam do?

Through disobeying the Word of God, he brought sin and death upon the human race.

What did Jesus the Messiah do?

He was the only Man who ever lived a sinless life and thus qualified to become the perfect atonement for sin, to redeem from Sheol (Hell) those Jewish saints. . .Abraham, Isaac, Jacob, David, Daniel, etc. . .who slept, and from eternal death and damnation those who lived after Him and who believed in Him.

The Anointed One, Jesus said:

> **"Truly, truly, I say to you, he who
> hears My word, and believes Him
> who sent Me, has eternal life, and
> does not come into judgment, but
> has passed out of death into life."**

> **(John 5:24)**

This is not just a promise for the future, some far-off distant time; it is a living promise that enters our lives the moment we believe on the Messiah. In that moment of faith, our beings pass from death unto life. . . .A stream of living water that flows from the Lord God through His Son, Messiah Jesus, cleanses us from all our sins.

The river of life which flows from the Eternal God into our spirits is explained this way:

> **For while we were still helpless, at the
> right time Christ died for the ungodly.
> For one will hardly die for a righteous
> man; though perhaps for the good man
> someone would dare even to die. But
> God demonstrates His own love to-**

> ward us, in that while we were yet
> sinners, Christ died for us. Much
> more then, having now been justi-
> fied by His blood, we shall be saved
> from the wrath of God through Him.
> For if while we were enemies, we
> were reconciled to God through the
> death of His Son, much more, hav-
> ing been reconciled, we shall be sav-
> ed by His life.

> **(Romans 5:6-10)**

LIVING WITHIN US

King David said, "No man can by any means redeem his brother, or give to God a ransom for him" (Psalm 49:7) . . .but from the moment of the Messiah's appearance upon this earth the whole concept of man's inevitable death changed and we hear the words:

> **"Death is swallowed up in victory.
> O death, where is your victory? O
> death, where is your sting?" The
> sting of death is sin, and the pow-
> er of sin is the law.**

> **(I Corinthians 15:54-56)**

> . . .I will redeem them from death.
> O Death, where are your thorns? O
> Sheol, where is your sting?. . .

> **(Hosea 13:14)**

What has caused this change in the attitude of the Scriptures, the words of God, regarding death?

One has come Who can stand and say, "I am. . .the living One; and I was dead, and behold, I am alive forevermore, and I have the keys of death and of Hades." (Revelation 1:17,18)

When Jesus the Messiah died on the cross, was resurrected from the dead on the third day, and ascended into Heaven to live forever in the presence of Almighty God, He took from Satan the keys of Hell and of death. Now the Messiah Jesus holds the eternal power over them.

King David saw this Messiah Who would have dominion over death when he wrote in the 23rd Psalm, verse 4:

> **Even though I walk through the valley of the shadow of death, I fear no evil; for Thou art with me; Thy rod and Thy staff, they comfort me.**

The list of references in both the Old and the New Testaments between the death caused by Adam and the life brought by the Messiah are many.

Jesus the Messiah said, "The thief comes only to steal, and kill, and destroy; I (the Messiah) came that they might have life, and might have it abundantly." (John 10:10)

> **For if by the transgression of the one, death reigned through the one, much more those who receive the abundance of grace and of the gift of righteousness will reign in life through the One, Jesus Christ. So then as through one transgression there resulted condemnation to all men, even so through one act of righteousness there resulted justification of life to all men.**
> **(Romans 5:17-18)**

Through the Second Adam we can defeat death which came by the first Adam and enter into eternal life which comes by the Messiah Jesus.

> **The last enemy that will be abolished is death.**
> **(I Corinthians 15:26)**

Chapter 13

A Night of Miracles

The Scriptures are full of miracles, many of which we have mentioned in these pages. We will also tell you of modern day miracles in the lives of men and women who have received supernatural help for their problem through the power of the resurrected Christ.

All of these miracles should set up a chain of questioning in our mind that leads us to the Source of such might and power.

To ask questions is not ignorance; it is wisdom.

> Make your ear attentive to wisdom,
> Incline your heart to understanding;
> For if you cry for discernment, Lift
> your voice for understanding; If you
> seek her as silver, And search for her
> as for hidden treasures; Then you
> will discern the fear of the LORD,
> And discover the knowledge of
> God.

(Proverbs 2:2-5)

I want to tell you of a man. . .a wise man. . .who was attracted by the signs and miracles which he observed in the ministry of Jesus. This man confessed his ignorance and lack of understanding and thereby had opened to him the way to receive the greatest miracle in all the world.

This wise man was named Nicodemus. He was a Pharisee, a ruler of the Jews. His dramatic story is told in the third chapter of the Gospel of John in the New Testament.

Though it was by night that he came to inquire of Jesus, nevertheless he accorded Him the respect and title of a master of Israel when he addressed Him.

"Rabbi," he said, "we know that you have come from God as a teacher; for no one can do these signs that You do unless God is with him."

His utterance is recorded as a statement of fact. . .but Jesus must have discerned that it was really a question, for the next verse, verse three. . .says that "Jesus *answered* and said to him. . . ."

What Jesus answered and said to him is the basis for the greatest miracle in all the world. . .greater than the healing of cancer, greater than the healing of the lame or the blind or the deaf, greater than the healing of heart trouble.

The most profound and far-reaching formula in all the world is contained in these simple words from Jesus:

> **"Truly, truly, I say to you, unless**
> **one is born again, he cannot see the**
> **kingdom of God."**

> **(John 3:3)**

Though Nicodemus was a learned master of Israel, he could not understand this statement at all.

However he did not feign understanding nor fake wisdom as the manner of many is. He came as a little child and inquired further.

"How can a man be born when he is old? He cannot enter a second time into his mother's womb and be born, can he?"

Gently, graphically, Jesus unfolded to the perplexed inquirer the meaning of the words.

"What is born of the flesh is flesh," He explained.

This means that those born of Adam are of Adam.

It takes us right back to the Garden of Eden where Adam brought forth children after his kind, in his image, under judgment and with the seed of death in himself.

What discouragement if that had been the end!

But Jesus didn't end His instruction at that point.

He added, *"That which is born of the Spirit is spirit."*

In effect, He was pointing out that though we were born of the flesh in the first Adam, in the Second Adam we can have a rebirth in the spirit.

Through Adam, we were alienated from our rightful place as sons through the creation. After Adam's fall, progeny was reckoned after the likeness of sinful Adam, not after the sinless image of God.

But God's love overcame that and He found a way.

If we as individuals could not be counted sons of God through His earthly son who failed, yet by taking our place in the Son Who overcame, we could experience a new birth and become a child of God in truth.

> **See how great a love the Father has bestowed upon us, that we should be called children of God . . .**
>
> **(I John 3:1)**

We become the sons of God through belief in and acceptance of the only begotten Son of God, Messiah.

> **For all who are being led by the Spirit of God, these are sons of God. For you have not received a spirit of slavery leading to fear again, but you have received a spirit of adoption as sons by which we cry out, "Abba! Father!" The Spirit Himself bears witness with our spirit that we are children of God, and if children, heirs also, heirs of God and fellow-heirs with Christ, if indeed we suf-**

> fer with Him in order that we may
> also be glorified with Him.
>
> (Romans 8:14-17)

> But when the fulness of the time
> came, God sent forth His Son, born
> of a woman, born unde the Law, in
> order that He might redeem those
> who were under the Law, that we
> might receive the adoption as sons.
> And because you are sons, God has
> sent forth the Spirit of His Son in-
> to our hearts, crying, "Abba! Fa-
> ther!" Therefore you are no lon-
> ger a slave, but a son; and if a son,
> then an heir through God.
>
> (Galatians 4:4-7)

We are born sons and daughters of Adam, yes! In his sin image, we live under the law of the flesh until the beautiful day we are reborn through faith in the Messiah and thus receive stamped upon our beings His divine image. We are made through Him the very elect children of God.

> Beloved, now we are children of God,
> and it has not appeared as yet what
> we shall be. We know that, when
> He appears, we shall be like Him,
> because we shall see Him just as He is.
>
> (I John 3:2)

What position and what power!

If you have never received Jesus as your Messiah, this moment could be the most important one of your life because right now you are faced with a choice of life or death.

> **There is a way which seems right**
> **to a man, But its end is the way**
> **of death.**

> ### (Proverbs 14:12)

Right now, you can begin to experience eternal life and peace with God in your innermost being by simply saying, "YES, I accept the Messiah; I accept the eternal life and the forgiveness of sins for which God's Son Jesus atoned through His death on the cross."

The Tabernacle of God is in your heart; you are sanctified through His blood. . .and, as God said, "I will also walk among you and be your God, and you shall be My people." (Leviticus 26:12)

The Messiah Jesus will make His habitation in your heart right now and will take away all your sins.

> **"But this is the covenant which I**
> **will make with the house of Israel**
> **after those days," declares the**
> **LORD, "I will put My law within**
> **them, and on their heart I will write**
> **it; and I will be their God, and they**
> **shall be My people."**

> ### (Jeremiah 31:33)

I believe the greatest miracle God can give to a person is the miracle of salvation.

It is yours, even now, very simply. . .

In fact, it is so simple that we could easily let it pass us by.

Faith is a fact. . .but faith is also an act.

Our part is simply to come, to believe, to receive.

God's part is to do the rest, to reveal the Messiah unto our hearts, to forgive our sins, to make us new.

Believe me, He will do it even now.

I invite you to pray this prayer with me right now.

Put both of your hands on this book as a point of contact and repeat this prayer out loud after me:

Lord God of Israel, Lord God of Abraham, Isaac and Jacob, I thank you for the full revelation of the Messiah to my hungry, searching heart.

Let me know by Thy divine Holy Spirit the One Who is the fulfillment of all the promises of redemption which You have given since the fall of Adam.

Right now I give myself to You!

Thank You for the forgiveness of sin through the atonement of Thy perfect Sacrifice, a Second Adam the Messiah Jesus.

I repent of my sins and I ask that through the redeeming work of the Messiah, His death, the shedding of His blood, that all my sins be forgiven me. Right Now!

I receive You, Jesus, into my life as Lord of my life, as the Savior of my soul, as my Messiah, the Son of the Living God!

With all my heart I praise You for the victory in my life. Amen.

As you have prayed this prayer sincerely, you can rest in confidence that a work has been done in your heart through the Second Adam and that you have been received by God through Him.

> **"All that the Father gives Me shall come to Me; and the one who comes to Me I will certainly not cast out."**
>
> **(John 6:37)**
>
> **"But as many as received Him, to them He gave the right to become**

children of God, even to those who
believe in His name,"

(John 1:12)

". . .if you confess with your mouth
Jesus as Lord, and believe in your
heart that God raised Him from the
dead, you shall be saved;"

(Romans 10:9)

"for with the heart man believes,
resulting in righteousness, and with
the mouth he confesses, resulting
in salvation."

(Romans 10:10)

Now I want you to go one step further with me.

To seal your commitment in your heart take this definite step of faith and on page 132 I have prepared a place for you to make and sign a spiritual commitment.

It is simply an act of affirming your new found faith in God.

You do not join anything.

You do not buy anything.

This is your personal act between you and God!

It will help you as you perform this definite act to affirm your commitment.

And now get ready for some very exciting news:

Chapter 14

Yesterday, Today, and Forever

Not only was our redemption from sin effected in the vicarious suffering of Jesus, but so was our healing from sicknesses and afflictions as pointed out in that verse. . . "by His scourging we are healed!"

The Psalmist David pointed out the benefits of God's healing power when he wrote in the 103rd Psalm, verses 2 and 3:

> **Bless the LORD, O my soul, And forget none of His benefits; Who pardons all your iniquities; Who heals all your diseases;**

Just as those who have experienced forgiveness of sin and are living lives of victory today are a witness to God's *saving* power, so we are seeing miracles of physical healing today. . .a visible witness to God's *healing* power.

The physical miracles witnessed by Jesus' disciples as they ministered in His name 2,000 years ago were visible proof that His words were true.

We read in Mark 16:20 in the New Testament:

> **And they went out and preached everywhere, while the Lord worked with them, and confirmed the word by the signs that followed.**

And in Hebrews 2:4, the Word says:

> **God also bearing witness with them, both by signs and wonders and by various miracles and by gifts of the Holy Spirit according to His own will.**

Jesus Himself admonished His hearers in John 10:37 and 38:

> **"If I do not do the works of My**
> **Father, do not believe Me; but if**
> **I do them, though you do not be-**
> **lieve Me, believe the works, that**
> **you may know and understand**
> **that the Father is in Me, and I in**
> **the Father."**

He promised His followers in Mark 16:17 that "these signs shall follow them that believe. . ." and that promise was not just for that time in which He was physically on earth. . .it is for every time and for every believer in Him.

God is the same yesterday, today and forever.

It is a great witness to the world today that Jesus is the Messiah and that He was resurrected from the dead when His resurrection power is revealed in physical healings as we pray in His Name.

I have been blessed to see great miracles of healing all over this world. . .among Indians, Africans, Jews, South Americans, Asians. . .wherever God has sent me as His servant with His message.

Many of these healings have been documented and appear regularly in a worldwide monthly publication called *Deeper Life*.

A few of the modern day miracles which we have seen as the result of our ministry in North America have been included in my book, *Miracles Happen When Someone Cares*.

Notable among these are those who have had cancer, "Devil's Pain," deafness, heart trouble, and other disabling problems.

Devil's Pain is the "easy" name for a disease known as tic douloureux, the degeneration of the trigeminal nerve which causes spasms of excruciating pain. Doctors have been unable to find a cure. . .but in the case of Jean Vickers of Clute, Texas, there *was* a cure. She was healed through faith in Jesus Christ, the Messiah.

Doctors tell us that nine out of ten people with Jean's problem try to commit suicide to get away from the terrible torment that is unreached even by the strongest medication. Jean herself was on the verge of suicide a number of times.

One night she was attending a meeting I was conducting in Sacramento, California. I didn't even pray for the sick that night. . .instead I preached a prophecy message on Israel's key role in world affairs and why the events transpiring in that new nation made me know that the Messiah had come, and indeed that we are living in the days of the end of time when He shall come again as prophesied in the Scriptures.

It was not a message on physical healing. . .but somehow Jean's heart reached out during that message and she experienced a dramatic healing *from that hour*. There was no display of emotion at the time. . .she simply returned to her room, poured out all her pain medicine and announced to her husband that she was healed. If she had not been healed and had no medicine, he reported, she would have been a screaming maniac before morning.

However, Jean never had another recurrence of the pain. I am still in touch with her at the time of this writing. . . more than seven years after she was healed.

That's how Jesus destroys the work of the devil!

There is also Randy Wright, formerly owner of a Lincoln-Mercury new car dealership in Boulder, Colorado, who was suddenly stricken with heart trouble and hardening of the arteries when he was only 35 years old.

The sudden heart attack turned Randy's life completely around. He was never to work another day in the auto agency. He was placed in the hospital in Denver where doctors put him on the strongest medicine available for his nerves plus several pills each day for thinning his blood.

After being released from the hospital in Denver, Randy traveled to Houston only to have another attack and be placed in the hospital there.

Randy surrendered his life to Christ as the Messiah while in the hospital, but his physical healing took place later during a special crusade I was conducting in Houston.

Randy says that God spoke to him and told him to come to the service on Tuesday night and that He would heal him then. He was so weak that it took several people to help him into the auditorium. This tired him so greatly that he sat down in the first seat he came to. . .which meant he was in the extreme back of the building, as far as he could be from where I was ministering.

Under the anointing of the Holy Spirit, I said, "Someone is being healed right now of a serious heart condition. Stand up wherever you are!"

Randy told me later, "No one had to tell me I was healed or to stand up. I can't explain how it felt, but I *felt* myself healed. I felt the healing power start at the top of my head and I felt it go into my heart and through my body on down into my legs. I stood right up stronger than I have ever been. I walked down the aisle and right up onto the platform."

I knew right away that Randy had experienced a miracle, and so did he.

Though he had had a cardiogram just a few days previously , Randy returned to his doctor for another test the very next day. . .and it showed absolutely nothing wrong with his heart. This has been eight years ago. I still hear from Randy who is still in excellent health.

Cletta Roberts came into my meeting in Denver, Colorado, in 1972 encased in a steel back brace and lying on a cot. She had been in what she terms a "living hell" for seven years, ever since she had injured her back lifting a sack of potatoes while working in a school cafeteria.

Those seven years were a nightmare of pain, surgery, hospitals, pills, inactivity and depression. Despite surgery for a ruptured disc and five for spinal fusions, despite potent pain pills, Cletta often would awaken in such pain that her husband would have to take her to the hospital at 1 or 2 o'clock in the morning for a pain-killing shot.

Surgeons tried without success to insert a steel rod in Cletta's back and she had another operation for the purpose of boring two holes in her head to desensitize the nerves. This also failed.

Cletta even contemplated suicide.

"Only faith in God and an understanding husband brought me through," she says today.

When Cletta was brought into the last service of the Denver crusade, she didn't believe that she would be healed. . . all she had was hope. Her disbelief was so great she thought that others who were being healed were "faking it."

The service was all but over. . .I was trying to dismiss it . . .when the Spirit of God spoke to me. I called out over the microphone, "There is a woman in the back wearing a brace who has a back problem. If she will bend over and touch her toes, God will heal her."

Cletta felt a "funny sensation." Not daring to hope that it was she who was being singled out, she went to the ladies' lounge, took off her brace. . .and began to touch her toes freely without pain.

There was great rejoicing when she reentered the auditorium holding her brace aloft to demonstrate what the living Messiah had done.

Rebecca Hager of Evergreen, Colorado, did not contemplate taking her own life. . .but she often felt she might kill someone else because of the tremendous pressure in her life caused by a severe hormone imbalance.

Without a hormone shot every ten days, Rebecca "went to pieces" and suffered tremendous depression. So severe was her need that Rebecca was given a year's supply of medication at a time. She carried some of the medicine and at least ten hypo needles with her everywhere she went.

Adding to her miseries were varicose veins, sinus attacks, and so many allergies that she had to wear a medical alert bracelet to be sure no one would administer the wrong kind of medicine. She also had a growth on her thyroid, suffered from arthiritis, and had a disabled arm.

Rebecca attended my crusade meetings and also the morning Holy Spirit Teaching Seminar sessions, but she did not come to be healed. She was just enjoying a "mountain top spiritual experience" as God revealed the power of the Messiah to her more and more.

Finally, on the last morning, I told the congregation that the power of the Messiah was present in a mighty way. I urged them to raise their hands and cast out everything from Satan, that what he tried to put on them did not belong to them; they could be rid of it in Jesus.

"I couldn't think what I wanted to be loosed from," Rebecca says now. "My mind was a compete blank. I didn't even think about my bondage to hormone shots."

However, as she stood there, the power of the Messiah was so real that her disabled arm was healed. The next morning she noticed that the growth on her neck had disappeared.

She felt sure that other problems had been solved also, but didn't mention it to anyone until long after the "ten-day" deadline for her hormone need had passed. . .and she felt absolutely no pressure. Her other ailments also were completely healed.

Rebecca called my office just a few days before this writing to tell of a planned trip to Africa and to praise God anew for what He has done for her.

Mildred Caddell had hands that looked like claws when she came to our Sixth World Deeper Life Conference in San Diego in 1971.

Crippled by osteo-arthritis, the hands were completely unusable. Mildred couldn't make a fist, hold a cup or even close thumb and forefinger together to pick up a needle.

The crippling disease had begun in 1950. By 1962 Mildred couldn't perform even the simplest household tasks. By 1967 large knots had developed on her wrists, she was suffering from chest pains and her arms "felt dead."

She began to feed on sugar coated aspirin, consuming three every four hours. Often she took as many as 18 aspirin in a 24 hour period. . .the maximum the doctors would allow her.

Mildred came to our Deeper Life Conference in 1967 expecting to be healed, but she became so caught up in the spiritual atmosphere she forgot all about her physical condition.

One afternoon, I had returned to my hotel room to rest while an associate was conducting an afternoon service in the auditorium. Suddenly God spoke to me and said, "Son, get up. My healing Spirit is being poured out this afternoon. Go and minister to My people."

I returned to the auditorium and told the people what God had revealed to me.

"There are 50 to 100 people in the auditorium suffering from arthritis, hearing problems and cataracts," I told them.

"If you will just stand up and take it, the Lord will heal you."

Here is what Mildred had to say later:

"Rev. Cerullo prayed and then I heard him say, 'Make a fist.' I did. . .the first one I had been able to make in years. I was crying with joy. My husband asked if I could really make a fist. . .so I made one. . .and hit him on the arm."

Mildred and her husband, Hughes, a retired Naval Commander, often attend my crusades now and both testify to the healing power of the risen Messiah. So compete is Mildred's healing that she has resumed her hobby of sewing and intricate needle work.

I am giving you all of these examples to tell you that the Messiah is real. It is He Who performs the miracles, not Morris Cerullo.

We have a saying. It is the banner over this ministry: "This is not the work of a man, but of the Holy Spirit of the Living God."

I want to give an example that clearly demonstrates that it is not myself who heals, but God Who is present everywhere and able to reach anyone.

It is the true story of Louise Judd, a widow who lives in the tiny little town of Russell Springs, Kentucky.

THE LOUISE JUDD STORY

Louise suffered so severely from Parkinson's Disease that she often thought her arm would shake out of the socket. Also, she had been totally, completely blind for two years.

An eye surgeon in Louisville told her that the blindness was caused by blood vessels breaking behind her eyeballs and that there was absolutely nothing that could be done to correct the condition.

Louise had never heard of me before, but one night around Thanksgiving of 1974, her son tuned into the Helpline television program which I was presenting. People in need were invited to call in for prayer and counseling. If they called our toll-free number, they could talk to one of my trained counselors right then.

Eddie called for his mother who talked and prayed with one of the counselors. At the end of the program, I led in a special prayer for all those in need who had called in during the evening.

That night Louise went to bed seeminly in the same condition she had been in. However, she wrote to me later, she woke up twice during the night and both times she was praying. When she awoke in the morning, the first thing she noticed was that her arm was not shaking.

Then she opened her eyes and saw daylight for the first time in two years! Her eyes were completely healed.

A member of my staff visited Louise to get her full story and we continue to keep in close touch with her.

Louise's dramatic miracle has been a source of witness of the power of Messiah to the entire town of Russell Springs and far beyond.

Hundreds and hundreds more such stories are located in my files. They are happening every day.

Why?

Because Jesus is Who He said He is, He is performing miracles *today* to manifest His resurrection power!

It is true that they took his body down from the cross on which He was crucified and laid it in a tomb. . .but that was not the end.

> **Now late on the Sabbath, as it began
> to dawn toward the first day of the
> week, Mary Magdalene and the other**

Mary came to look at the grave. And
behold, a severe earthquake had occurred, for an angel of the Lord de-
scended from heaven and came and
rolled away the stone and sat upon
it. And his appearance was like light-
ning, and his garment as white as
snow; and the guards shook for fear
of him, and became like dead men.
And the angel answered and said to
the women, "Do not be afraid; for I
know that you are looking for Jesus
who has been crucified. "He is not
here, for He has risen, just as He said.
Come, see the place where He was lying. "And go quickly and tell His disciples that He has risen from the dead;
and behold, He is going before you into Galilee, there you will see Him; behold, I have told you." And they de-
parted quickly from the tomb with
fear and great joy and ran to report
it to His disciples. And behold, Jesus
met them and greeted them. And
they came up and took hold of His
feet and worshiped Him. Then Jesus
said to them, "Do not be afraid; go
and take word to My Brethren to
leave for Galilee, and there they shall
see Me."

(Matthew 28:1-10)

After this, according to Paul's writings, Jesus was seen
on a number of occasions.

For I delivered to you as of first importance what I also received, that
Christ died for our sins according to

the Scriptures, and that He was buried, and that He was raised on the third day according to the Scriptures, and that He appeared to Cephas, then to the twelve. After that He appeared to more than five hundred brethren at one time, most of whom remain until now, but some have fallen asleep; then He appeared to James, then to all the apostles; and last of all, as it were to one untimely born, He appeared to me also.

(I Corinthians 15:3-8)

He was seen by several hundred disciples as He ascended into heaven some days after His resurrection from the dead:

And after He had said these things, He was lifted up while they were looking on, and a cloud received Him out of their sight.

(Acts 1:9)

Before He ascended, however, Jesus made many promises to His disciples, both of that day and to all those who were to follow, regarding His Presence with them and His power which would be manifested in their lives because of His finished work of redemption.

Jesus came into this world to destroy the works of the devil.

In Him we have forgiveness of sin.

In Him we have healing for our bodies.

Both sin and sickness are from Satan and came as a result of the fall and disobedience of the first Adam.

Best of all now in the Messiah we have eternal life, for He tore away the pangs of death when He became the first-fruits of the resurrection.

. . .All this through the obedience of the Second Adam! Isaiah prophesied:

> **He will swallow up death for all time,**
>
> **(Isaiah 25:8)**

> **". . .DEATH IS SWALLOWED UP**
> **IN VICTORY. "O DEATH, WHERE**
> **IS YOUR VICTORY? O DEATH,**
> **WHERE IS YOUR STING?"**
>
> **(I Corinthians 15:54-55)**

> **Jesus said to her, "I am the resurrec-**
> **tion and the life; he who believes in**
> **Me shall live even if he dies,**
>
> **(John 11:25)**

The Messiah has accomplished His purpose by His victory over Satan, by His death on the cross and His resurrection from the dead!

However, His purpose is accomplished in *us* only when we accept the atonement, healing, and life eternal He offers.

> **"Come now, and let us reason to-**
> **gether," Says the LORD, "Though**
> **your sins are as scarlet, They will be**
> **as white as snow; Though they**
> **are red like crimson, They will be**
> **like wool.**
>
> **(Isaiah 1:18)**

This is the means of destroying the works of the enemy in every aspect of our lives. He is defeated through the Messiah!

"BLESS the LORD, O my soul; And
all that is within me, bless His holy
name. Bless the LORD, O my soul,
And forget none of His benefits;
Who pardons all your iniquities;
Who heals all your diseases;"

(Psalm 103:1-3)

As the Holy Spirit has witnessed the challenge of the Messiah through the message in this book, will you not take a simple step of faith now and fill out your confidential commitment on the next page?

⟶

[Editor's note: All healing testimonies referred to in this book are documented, verified healings which are standing to this day. All case histories and collaboration are on file at Morris Cerullo World Evangelism Headquarters, San Diego, CA 92138.]

A Challenge

MY COMMITMENT TO THE MESSIAH — JESUS!

This is to certify that on this date _____ I accept Jesus of Nazareth as my Messiah. I see in the Scriptures that He fulfills the prophecies spoken about the Messiah.

I accept Him as the Second Adam Who restores to me all the dominion and rights lost to me in first Adam.

I do declare that Jesus is the living Messiah, the Son of God and that through His Name I received the miracle of salvation, the gift of the new birth.

I believe He receives me now just as I am and gives me the power to become a child of God.

> **"And there is salvation in no one else;
> for there is no other name under hea-
> ven that has been given among men,
> by which we must be saved."**
>
> **(Acts 4:12)**

_____
(Signed)

_____
(Date)

This is your commitment between you and the Lord. Keep in this book as your personal reminder.

A Postscript

Now that you have accepted Jesus of Nazareth as the Messiah, you have eaten of the Bread of Life. In fact, you have *entered* a new life.

That life needs sustenance.

This great joy can be maintained and sustained as we live our lives fully in Messiah and are sustained by His strength daily.

One of the important things lost by man in the first Adam and reclaimed in the Second Adam is face to face communion with God.

We may come boldly before His throne daily:

> Let us therefore draw near with con-
> fidence to the throne of grace, that
> we may receive mercy and may find
> grace to help in time of need.
>
> (Hebrews 4:16)
>
> But we all, with unveiled face behold-
> ing as in a mirror the glory of the
> Lord, are being transformed into the
> same image from glory to glory, just
> as from the Lord, the Spirit.
>
> (2 Corinthians 3:18)

Another vital ingredient of continuing to live a victorious life in Messiah is fellowship with others who also know Him and love Him:

> Then those who feared the LORD
> spoke to one another, and the
> LORD gave attention and heard it,
> and a book of remembrance was
> written before Him for those who
> fear the LORD and who esteem His

> name. "And they will be Mine," says
> the LORD of hosts, "on the day that I
> prepare My own possession, and I will
> spare them as a man spares his own
> son who serves him."

> **(Malachi 3:16-17)**

> not forsaking our own assembling
> together, as is the habit of some,
> but encouraging one another; and
> all the more, as you see the day
> drawing near.

> **(Hebrews 10:25)**

Remember also that life is sustained by "bread." The Word of God is our daily bread and our staff of life. We must eat daily.

> . . .that He might make you under-
> stand that man does not live by
> bread alone, but man lives by every-
> thing that proceeds out of the mouth
> of the LORD.

> **(Deuteronomy 8:3)**

In these pages I have touched on fragments of the precious truths to be found in the pages of God's Word. There is more. . .much more. . .and a systematic study of God's Word will reveal the Messiah to your heart more and more.

BIBLE CORRESPONDENCE COURSE

For this purpose, I am offering you the opportunity to take part in an absolutely free Bible Correspondence Course. This is the English version of a similar course prepared in Hebrew in which more than 25,000 Jews in Israel are enrolled.

Fill out the special tear-out page in the back of this book and mail it today to receive the first lesson of the free Bible Correspondence Course. There is absolutely *no obligation* and absolute confidentiality is assured.

Also, please write to me!

Not only do I want to hear the good news that you have found Jesus as your Messiah, but I want to pray with you for any requests or needs you may have.

Every Friday is a day of prayer and fasting at our headquarters office here in San Diego. No matter where I am, I join our staff in this day of fasting and prayer for the needs of people worldwide. Many of my staff join me in this special time to pray for the needs of our friends. We would like to include you in our very special prayer time.

One of my favorite Scriptures is the verse in Matthew 18:19, which says:

> "...that if two of you agree on earth
> about anything that they may ask, it
> shall be done for them by My Father
> who is in heaven."

I will be happy to pray with you for any need you may have. Our God is interested and concerned about every detail of your life, whether it is spiritual, physical, a family need for mother, father, children, grandparents, or even friends, for your financial and business needs. . .in fact, every facet of your life. God is relevant and at the point of our need.

Whatever your needs, write to me today. I will be waiting to hear.

> May the LORD answer you in the
> day of trouble! May the name of the
> God of Jacob set you securely on
> high! May He send you help from
> the sanctuary, And support you from

Zion! May He remember all your
meal offerings, And find your burnt
offering acceptable! May He grant
you your heart's desire, And fulfill
all your counsel! We will sing for joy
over your victory, And in the name
of our God we will set up our ban-
ners. May the LORD fulfill all your
petitions.

(Psalm 20:1-5)

In the Name of the Messiah, Jesus.

Your friend and God's servant,

Morris Cerullo

AN ANSWER TO MANY QUESTIONS!

BESORAT SHALOM (A Gospel of Peace)

Hear the words of the Prophets come alive in "Besorat Shalom" a Bible Correspondence Course that speaks plainly about the true meaning of the ancient manuscripts.

Yours free and without any obligation

*Offers the convenience and privacy of study in your own home.

*The guarantee of confidence that your privacy shall never be violated.

*No calls will be made and no follow-up materials other than what you request.

25,000 currently enrolled.

SENT FREE & WITHOUT OBLIGATION

Mark the box on response form inside back cover and mail today.

SPECIAL BONUS WITH FIRST LESSON

HAVE YOU EVER NEEDED A MIRACLE?

12 Thrilling Documented testimonies of how God met people at their point of need!

MARGUERITE had massive surgery — but Cancer was still there!

RANDY was a successful businessman. . .until his heart gave way.

JEAN went into the garage to hang herself. . .

Morris Cerullo has compiled a collection of some of the outstanding miracles of our time. Many years in the making, *MIRACLES HAPPEN*, contains 12 well documented case stories of people who reached out to God in the hour of their need. . . .

Faith Building. . . .Perhaps a miracle could happen to you at your point of need while you are reading this 110 page book!

Read how their active faith made possible their impossibilities.

Mark response form inside back cover and mail today!

"I am the Lord thy God that

"He sent his word, and healed them, and

Jewish Family Healed in Pasadena

Triple Miracle For Jewish Family

One of the highlights of the Morris Cerullo Crusade in Pasadena, California was the healing of a Jewish family from Beverly Hills. Mrs. Cole, her daughter Lisa, and son Rick had accepted Jesus as their Messiah, but all suffered serious afflictions.

All three received outstanding miracles at the same time. The mother suffered with an acute sinus condition since she was 12 years of age. Surgery had failed to correct the condition. All of a sudden she had felt her nose dry up for the first time. She had been coughing all through the service and it just stopped. She turned to her daughter who could not read without her glasses. All of a sudden, Lisa's vision cleared and she demonstrated on the platform that she could read very fine print without difficulty. Rick also was healed of an acute sinus condition.

UNFORGETTABLE SIGHT

The sight of all three Jews on the platform, crying and hugging each other, was something that I shall never forget. The praise and thanksgiving went up to God from nearly everyone in the audience as they shared the joy of this family over their multiple miracle.

healeth thee " **Exodus 15:26**

delivered them from their destructions"
Psalm 107:20

Stroke Victim Healed in Denver

A stroke and advice from a Jewish husband.

Bernice Zwibecker, had been a very sad person when she entered the crusade auditorium, in Denver, in September of 1972 on the first night. A stroke had paralyzed nearly half of her body and had sapped most of the strength out of what had remained for her to use.

Her Jewish husband had seen one of the crusade advertisements and had told her she should make the supreme effort required to attend. . . .For Bernice it was, "What have I got to loose?"

All she lost was pain and misery, for she felt the healing power of God go through her body and restore every muscle to its rightful place and function. Her face that had so sadly drooped on one side was now perfectly normal. Since this miracle experience, her whole life has been revolutionized.

GOD WILL HEAL YOU! "Who forgiveth all thine iniquities; who healeth all thy diseases" (Psalm 103:3 KJV)

I want to pray personally for you. Send me your request today.

Morris Cerullo

Appendix

SUMMATION OF SCRIPTURES

COMPARISONS IN SCRIPTURE

1. ADAM WAS CREATED IN THE IMAGE AND LIKENESS OF GOD.

Genesis 1:26, 27 Old Testament: Then God said, "Let Us make man in Our image, according to Our likeness; and let them rule over the fish," etc. Verse 26. And God created man in His own image. . .Verse 27.

1. CHRIST IS THE EXACT AND ETERNAL REVELATION OF JEHOVAH GOD.

Colossians 1:15 New Testament: And He is the image of the invisible God. . .

Hebrews 1:3 New Testament: And He is the radiance of His glory and the exact representation of His nature. . .

John 14:9 New Testament: He who has seen Me has seen the Father. . .

2. ADAM WAS CREATED TO BE GOD'S COMPANION.

Genesis 1:26 Old Testament: NOTE VERSE: ". . .according to Our likeness. . ." in interests as well as appearance.

Genesis 3:8 Old Testament: ". . .the man and his wife hid themselves. . ." and

Genesis 3:24 Old Testament: "drove. . .out. . ." Fellowship with Jehovah broken.

2. CHRIST HAS ALWAYS BEEN GOD'S COMPANION.

Philippians 2:6 New Testament: Who, being in the form of God, thought it not robbery to be equal with God: (KJV)

John 17:5 New Testament: "And now, glorify Thou Me together with Thyself, Father, with the glory which I ever had with Thee before the world was.

3. ADAM WAS FORMED OF THE EARTH. HE WAS EARTHY.

Genesis 2:7 Old Testament: . . .dust from the ground. . .

I Corinthians 15:47 New Testament. . .from the earth. . .

3. CHRIST IS THE MESSIAH, LORD FROM HEAVEN, NOT EARTH.

John 8:42 New Testament: ". . .for I proceeded forth and have come from God, for I have not even come on My own initiative, but He sent Me."

Isaiah 7:14 Old Testament: Therefore the Lord Himself will give you a sign: Behold, a virgin will be with child and bear a son, and she will call His name Immanuel.

Hebrews 10:5 New Testament:. . .BUT A BODY THOU HAST PREPARED FOR ME;

I Corinthians 15:47 New Testament: The first man is from the earth, earthy; the second man is from heaven.

4. ADAM RECEIVED HIS LIFE FROM GOD.

Genesis 2:7 Old Testament: . . .breathed into his nostrils the breath of life. . .

4. CHRIST HIMSELF THE LIFE OF GOD.

I John 5:12 New Testament: He who has the Son has the life. . .

I Corinthians 15:45 New Testament: So also it is written, "The first MAN, Adam, BECAME A LIVING SOUL." The last Adam became a life-giving spirit.

5. ADAM WAS GIVEN A WORLD-WIDE DOMINION.

Genesis 1:28 Old Testament: . . .God said. . .". . .rule . . . over every living thing that moves on the earth."

Genesis 1:29 Old Testament: Then God said, "Behold, I have given you every plant yielding seed that is on the surface of all the earth. . ."

Genesis 2:19 Old Testament: . . .what he would call them . . .that was its name.

5. CHRIST AS A MAN EXERCISED THIS AUTHORITY.

Mark 11:2, 7-10 New Testament: (read all) An unbroken colt passively carried Him.

Matthew 17:27 New Testament: The fish were prompt to serve Him.

Matthew 21:18-19 New Testament: The trees were subject to Him.

Matthew 8:26-27 New Testament: The elements themselves obeyed His will.

6. ADAM THROUGH DISOBEDIENCE LOST HIS GREAT AUTHORITY.

Genesis 3:17 Old Testament: . . ."Cursed is the ground because of you. . ."

Genesis 3:18 Old Testament: "Both thorns and thistles it shall grow for you. . ."

Genesis 3:24 Old Testament: So He drove the man out. . .

6. CHRIST THROUGH OBEDIENCE SHALL FOREVER RETAIN AND INCREASE HIS DOMAIN.

Isaiah 9:7 Old Testament: There will be no end to the increase. . .

Isaiah 11:4-16 Old Testament: But with righteousness He will judge the poor, And decide with fairness for the afflicted. . .the wolf will dwell with the lamb, And the leopard will lie down with the kid. . .And a little boy will lead them. . . .For the earth will be full of the knowledge of the Lord. . .in that day

That the nations will resort to the root of Jesse, Who will stand as a signal for the peoples; And His resting place will be glorious. Then it will happen on that day that the Lord Will again recover the second time with His hand The remnant of His people, who will remain, From Assyria, Egypt, Pathros, Cush, Elam, Shinar, Hamath, And from the islands of the sea. . . . .And will assemble the banished ones of Israel, And will gather the dispersed of Judah From the four corners of the earth.

Isaiah 12:1-6 THEN you will say on that day, "I will give thanks to Thee, O LORD; For although Thou wast angry with me, Thine anger is turned away. . .Behold, God is my salvation, I will trust and not be afraid; For the LORD God is my strength and song, And He has become my salvation. Therefore you will joyously draw water From the springs of salvation. . . .in that day you will say, "Give thanks to the LORD, call on His name. Make known His deeds among the peoples; Make them remember that His name is exalted." Praise the LORD in song. . .Cry aloud and shout for joy, O inhabitant of Zion, For great in your midst is the Holy One of Israel.

Yes, of His Kingdom there shall be no end. It is interpreted — "Immanuel — Christ — the Messiah — God with us.

OUR PLACE SCRIPTURALLY

1. IN ADAM WE ARE ALL SINNERS.

Romans 5:12 New Testament: . . .through one man sin entered into the world. . .

Romans 5:19 New Testament: For as through the one man's disobedience the many were made sinners. . .

1. IN CHRIST WE ARE MADE RIGHTEOUS.

Romans 5:19 New Testament: . . .so through. . .One the many will be made righteous.

II Corinthians 5:21 New Testament. . .we. . .become the righteousness of God in Him.

2. IN ADAM WE ARE DOOMED TO DEATH.

Genesis 2:17 Old Testament: ". . .not eat. . .surely die."

Genesis 3:6 Old Testament: . . .and he ate.

Genesis 5:5 Old Testament: . . .and he [Adam] died.

I Corinthians 15:22 New Testament: . . .in Adam all die. . . .

2. IN CHRIST WE POSSESS ETERNAL LIFE.

Romans 5:21 New Testament: . . .eternal life through Jesus Christ our Lord.

Romans 6:11 New Testament: . . .alive to God in Christ Jesus.

I Corinthians 15:22 New Testament. . .in Christ all shall be made alive.

Romans 5:12 New Testament: Therefore, just as through one man sin entered into the world, and death through sin, and so death spread to all men, because all sinned—

3. IN ADAM WE ARE SEPARATED FOR GOD.

Genesis 3:24 Old Testament: So He drove the man out. . .

Isaiah 59:2 Old Testament: But your iniquities have made a separation. . .His face. . .

Ephesians 2:12 New Testament: . . .you were. . .separate . . .excluded. . .strangers. . .

4. IN ADAM WE PARTAKE OF OUR FALLEN NATURE.

Genesis 5:3 Old Testament: . . .Adam. . .became the father of a son in his own likeness. . .

Ephesians 2:2 New Testament. . .sons of disobedience.

5. IN ADAM WE ARE BOUND TO CONSTANT TURMOIL. NO REST.

Genesis 3:19 Old Testament: By the sweat of your face You shall eat bread. . .

3. BUT IN CHRIST WE ARE BROUGHT BACK TO GOD.

Ephesians 2:13 New Testament:. . .in Christ Jesus you . . .have been brought near. . .

I Peter 3:18 New Testament: . . .Christ. . .died. . .might bring us to God. . .

4. IN CHRIST WE ARE PARTAKERS OF HIS DIVINE NATURE.

II Peter 1:4 New Testament: . . .partakers of the divine nature. . .

II Corinthians 5:17 New Testament: . . .in Christ. . .a new creature. . .

I John 3:2 New Testament: . . .now we are children of God. . .

5. IN CHRIST WE ARE NOW FREE TO ENJOY ETERNAL REST.

Hebrews 4:3 New Testament: For we who have believed enter that rest. . .

Isaiah 57:20 Old Testament: . . .wicked are like the tossing sea. . .cannot be quiet. . .

Matthew 11:28 New Testament: "Come. . .all who are weary and heavy laden, and I will give you rest.

Ephesians 2:4-6 New Testament: But God, being rich in mercy. . .even when we were dead in our transgressions, made us alive together with Christ. . .in the heavenly places. . .With our MESSIAH—CHRIST, THE SON OF GOD.

6. IN ADAM WE ARE CONDEMNED TO JUDGMENT.

Romans 5:18 New Testament: So then as through one transgression there resulted condemnation to all men. . .

6. IN CHRIST WE ARE ASSURED OF ETERNAL GLORY—NO FEAR OF THE JUDGMENT.

Romans 5:18b New Testament: even so through one act of righteousness there resulted justification of life to all men.

Romans 8:1 New Testament: . . .THERE is therefore now no condemnation for those who are in Christ Jesus.

ACKNOWLEDGEMENT: Biblical quotations, unless otherwised noted, are from New American Standard Bible by permission of Lockman Foundation, La Habra, California. The Lockman Foundation 1960, 1962, 1963, 1968, 1971

FROM THE DESK OF MORRIS CERULLO

Dear Reader,

This book is the culmination of many years of long hard research and revelation. Its purpose is to present in clear understandable language the parallels of truth in the written covenanted Word of God.

Too long people have been uncertain as to the meaning behind a great portion of the Holy Scriptures, Scriptures that might hold the keys to the greatest treasures available on this earth!

I trust that this book has been more than just another informative dissertation of the law. . .but rather that it has brought new life and meaning to ancient truths that have never ceased to operate. . . truths that even today are at work stirring people in their hearts.

Not knowing your faith, I ask you please not to feel offended at receiving this book. No ulterior motives were intended whatsoever. That is why it has come to you as a free gift.

I pray that you have read it in the Spirit of love in which I sent it.

My prayer is that you have read this book with an open mind and an open heart to the abundant blessings that are available to you.

The Author,

Morris Cerullo

P.S. I am very interested in your reaction to this book. . . .Many have been asking me to write this for sometime. Let me know if it proves to be a blessing to you.

(I have provided an envelope for this purpose.)